A YEAR OF PROGRAMS FOR
MILLENNIALS
AND MORE

A YEAR OF PROGRAMS FOR

MILLENNIALS

AND MORE

AMY J. ALESSIO \ KATIE LAMANTIA \ EMILY VINCI

ala
editions

An imprint of the American Library Association
Chicago 2015

© 2015 by the American Library Association

Extensive effort has gone into ensuring the reliability of the information in this book; however, the publisher makes no warranty, express or implied, with respect to the material contained herein.

ISBN: 978-0-8389-1332-1 (paper)

Library of Congress Cataloging-in-Publication Data
Alessio, Amy J.
    A year of programs for millennials and more / by Amy Alessio, Katie LaMantia, Emily Vinci.
        pages cm
    Includes bibliographical references and index.
    ISBN 978-0-8389-1332-1 (print : alk. paper) 1. Libraries—Activity programs—United States.
2. Generation Y—United States. I. LaMantia, Katie. II. Vinci, Emily, 1988– III. Title.
    Z716.33.A44 2015
    025.5—dc23
                                                                                            2015002616

Cover design by Kimberly Thornton. Imagery © Shutterstock, Inc.
Text design and composition by Alejandra Diaz in the Charis SIL and Brandon Grotesque typefaces.

♾ This paper meets the requirements of ANSI/NISO Z39.48–1992 (Permanence of Paper).

Printed in the United States of America
19 18 17 16 15   5 4 3 2 1

DEDICATION

*For my family and the library patrons and staff
who continue to inspire us.*
–AA–

*For my family and friends who have always
been there for me, and the library community
and patrons—it is an honor to work with you.*
–KL–

*For my family for their unending support
and encouragement and my patrons for their
enthusiasm and helpful feedback.*
–EV–

CONTENTS

ACKNOWLEDGMENTS

We thank the staff and patrons of the Schaumburg Township (Illinois) District Library for being so supportive of our programming and library.

INTRODUCTION

Welcome to *A Year of Programs for Millennials and More*. The programs in this manual are designed for young adults in their late teens, 20s, 30s, and 40s. It also suggests ways to reach out to these groups, market the programs, and bring these patrons into your library. Some programming, such as programs on job searches, will always draw people from all of these groups, but each of these groups will have specific frames of reference, needs, desires, and takeaway goals for the program. For example, people in their 30s with young children will have different information needs than those who are single in their 30s. Let's think more about each of these groups and the events typically happening in their lives.

Not Quite Teens, Not Quite Adults

The tumultuous high school years and late teen years are a busy time: school, sports, friends, social media, getting a driver's license, boyfriends, girlfriends, college, first jobs, and generally discovering who you are. It is the beginning stage of independence for many in this age group whether they are still in high school or recent graduates. Although libraries have traditionally offered teen programs, they have often been more successful at capturing the interests of the middle-school crowd. Capturing the 15–20 demographic is a challenge that goes beyond offering study spaces, booktalks, and craft programs; it's about capitalizing on their interests and making them see that the library goes beyond academics.

Changing the way teens view the library is no easy feat. But you can use programming topics teens are already highly engaged with that will offer teens a chance to socialize with their friends. Pop culture and nostalgia programs such as Throwback Halloween Night and Karaoke Night are easily adaptable and will engage older teens and create fun memories with friends. By associating more social and engaging events with the library, teens will keep coming back to the library as adults.

Many high school students are also looking for ways to positively change the world, and others simply need to fulfill volunteer hours. The Service Club, LGBT Pride Month, Memorial Day Service Fair, and Social Justice and Activism programs all provide service and volunteer options, plus they highlight great causes in the community that people may not be aware of. Create opportunities and a learning environment that expand teens' worldviews; you never know what issue or organization will spark an interest.

The majority of older teenagers are still enrolled in high school or college and spend most of their time at school. Stay connected with counselors, teachers, and the school board to share information and learn about the interests of teens in your community. If there is a community college within the library's service borders, coordinate with the librarian(s) to provide on-campus programming. The Community College Connections Club, presented later in this book, has a year of ideas for programming, and many can be adapted to suit high school students' needs. Visiting the high school and college campuses is critical to making library connections for both the students and librarians.

Totally 20s

The years between the ages of 20 and 29 are full of excitement and immense change. Any group of people in their 20s are likely to be in wildly different places in their lives—somewhere amid graduating from college and possibly graduate school, establishing careers, getting married, having babies, relocating, and, generally, figuring out how to be adults. Chances are a place they are *not* is at the library. That's not to say that people in their 20s don't use the public library at all. However, it's not typically the first place they look for relevant programs and events. Most people in their 20s are plenty comfortable with technology and its various uses, they have a social scene and have developed means for exploring their interests, and they consume culture in myriad ways. All of which is to say, you cannot necessarily expect those in the 20s demographic to come to you. You must go to them.

A huge part of meeting the social, informational, and entertainment needs of your 20s patrons is to meet them where they are. In terms of disseminating information, this means creating and making use of a presence on social media. Websites are great, but they are for people who already know about the programming in your library and are just looking for the facts. Using sites like Facebook and Twitter will allow the patrons you're already reaching to share the information with their friends and spread the word so others can discover your programming.

Several of the programs outlined in this book are great for off-site settings (Trivia Nights, Winery Tour and Tasting, and the Young Adult Books for Youngish Adults Club). Creating partnerships with local establishments is a great way not only to strengthen your library's ties to the community but also to reach potential patrons who may never set foot in the library. Instead of waiting for these people to come to the library, bring the library to them through off-site programming.

Programs geared toward people in their 20s need to have a social element as well. It can be difficult for a lot of people to make friends once out of the college environment, so a key element of creating successful library programs is making sure that the programs fill that need. The library can be a space to meet like-minded people, and programming should provide an opportunity for people to meet and get to know each other. The opportunities for socializing are obvious in programs like '90s Night and the Trivia Night series, but less obvious is something straightforward like Clutter Doctor. Still, creating a comfortable environment that encourages socializing is possible no matter what the program.

Trending for 30s

Folks in their 30s can be part of a few different groups: single professionals, married professionals, and parents (married or single). All have different needs, but few 30s have a lot of time to spare. They are used to downloading and accessing what they need online quickly. Many single 30s use online dating as a resource to meet people. Many have, or need to change, jobs and careers. Because people in their 30s are in such different places in their lives, each person will have unique library needs.

Online or frequent live demonstrations from the library that will easily fit into busy schedules will appeal to patrons in their 30s. Because of scheduling conflicts, the dad of two young children may not attend a program on how to download audiobooks onto his phone, but a handout and a quick demonstration that he can access while he's waiting in line to check out will help him.

All library resources save patrons money, but folks in their 30s will enjoy some services in particular. Those with children will enjoy free movies at night or on weekends, though they might not be able to attend regularly. Singles and married folks will enjoy free classes on things they have been meaning to try, but may not want to spend money on until they know they like it. It is important that these programs also have a social aspect because attendees will appreciate meeting others in their own age category and, especially, in a similar place in their life.

Many people in this age group may be new to the community. They might have moved to the area for a job or are buying their first home in the library community. These folks may not have a strong history with the area and do not know where to go for information on local preschools, 5K races, or volunteer opportunities. Several programs in this book help connect new community members in this age group to groups they will enjoy.

Juggling and Happy in the 40s

It can be a mistake to assume that all adults over a certain age enjoy the same topics at the library. Folks in their 40s could be parents of young children or tweens and teens. They could have college-age children. They could be caring for elderly parents. They could be struggling with divorce, layoffs, and more. They could be single and looking for ways to travel or invest. Many may have a bucket list of things they want to do before they turn 50 or before they retire. The library can make their life easier.

For example, searching on the Internet may not help connect these folks to healthy living. People in this group may also be self-conscious and need a comfortable environment in which to find the information they need. For example, the Fit Fair, 5K Club, and other programs in this book might not work well for people in their 40s who want to get into running if the program is filled with 20-somethings who run several marathons each year. But a Fit Fair or 5K Club just for people in their 40s can provide a good support group and a place to gather nonjudgmental information on health and running.

Even if people in their 40s are well informed about their own health, they may need to access information for other age groups. Someone in her 40s may do Iron

Man races each year yet need to know the latest research on health care or elder care for her parents. Making health resources and information on local senior living choices readily available for the person who is running in to get DVDs or looking on the website will help those in this age group.

Parenting doesn't get easier with age, and often new parents in their 40s may be older than other parents at school, and the library can be a place to meet other parents their age. People in their 40s with both young and older children will need to find programs for both age groups. Are all youth programs grouped together? Consider breaking them down by age in brochures and making them searchable by age on websites. The Parent Nights Club in this manual also discusses ways to introduce parents of young children to the library. Programs for entire families or service opportunities for the entire family may appeal to this age group.

Regardless of technology, the library is always a community center. People in their 40s may have fewer opportunities to make friends than other groups because of their many responsibilities. Programs targeted to 40s and advertised for people in their 30s and 40s will help provide opportunities for people in their 40s to meet new people and keep their social life active, while encouraging them to keep coming to the library for themselves as well as their families.

All the groups have library needs in common. The Youth Services group in your library likely already offers programs targeted for particular grades or ages. In the same way, adults have different issues and will benefit from targeted events when possible.

Why Should You Offer Programs for These Groups?

The Schaumburg Township (Illinois) District Library has had an active Teen Advisory Board (TAB) for sixteen years, started and run by Amy Alessio with other staff. In fact, Katie LaMantia was a teen member of the Teen Advisory Board at the library from the ages of 12 to 18. As a former TAB member, she fondly remembers participating in many of the fun social and volunteer activities at the library. However, after graduating from high school she did not come back to the public library until after graduating from college. When she became the teen librarian at the library, she began to notice this same trend among graduating teens.

A team of three librarians and a manager, including Katie LaMantia and Emily Vinci, met to address this growing issue. One of the biggest problems the group identified was the lack of programming to engage people in their 20s and 30s. As a result of this series of meetings, the NextGen group was formed to create a brand and a series of programs to target people in their 20s and 30s at the Schaumburg Township District Library. In October 2013, NextGen—"a social group for people in their 20s and 30s"—officially launched with a Throwback Halloween program quite similar to the one described in this book. Turnout for the program exceeded expectations, and the group continued to take form with a logo, a Facebook group, an e-newsletter, and a website.

NextGen now holds two to three programs a month, including a bimonthly book club and a monthly trivia night. Peppered among those are stand-alone programs designed to fit into the themes identified by the NextGen team as important and relevant to this demographic, such as pop culture/entertainment, education/information, hobby/DIY, and personal growth. Throughout all NextGen programs, the team strives to create a social, participatory experience.

The Schaumburg Township District Library has benefited from the NextGen program and from engaging these groups in several ways. Several programs are offered out in the community at coffee shops, community and college campuses, craft stores, or restaurants. These locations attract new people, who then come to the library to attend more events and to register. NextGen patrons often use social media and make posts or publish photos to their friends, further promoting the library. The NextGen collection has increased fiction circulation as well as popular nonfiction in the featured categories. The collection and displayed titles have materials on events nearby, which promotes programs again. We often hear from this group that they "had no idea the library had events for people in their age group."

This book will offer ideas for monthly themed clubs as well as individual program ideas for each month. The ideas for monthly clubs are designed for short sessions, while the individual programs include details from shopping lists to setup steps and marketing. Some programs are targeted to a specific age subgroup and will specify who may get the most out of the event.

How can a public library specify age groups for a program? The authors of this book all have experience working with designated ages within the library. Although a few patrons may not be happy that they are not invited to attend a particular event, those who are will get much more out of the experience from interacting with others in the appropriate age range. People in their 20s and 30s may be turned off by events that draw mostly folks in their 60s and 80s and vice versa. Older teens may find little in common with people in their 40s. It is always possible to offer a program more than once, making changes to accommodate more of the public if desired. Under the Variations heading in each program, we suggest options to make that program relevant to other age groups.

How to Use This Book

Each chapter begins with an introduction to the month and an overview of the programs, including a brief discussion of why those programs work well at that time of year. Under each month, programming ideas are listed. Details for these stand-alone events are provided under the following headings.

PREPARATION TIME

The preparation time estimate incorporates marketing, shopping, and setting up. It does not indicate just the time that will be spent preparing on the day of the event;

rather, it includes the entire time that will likely be spent planning. This will vary depending on the size of the library and the number of attendees and on whether marketing is handled by other staff in the library.

LENGTH OF PROGRAM

Program length is an estimate of how much time will be needed to complete the listed activities.

NUMBER OF PATRONS

This is intended to be an optimal number for the event. Each situation is different, and activities can be adjusted. Everyone has experienced both the program with unexpectedly huge attendance and the event with only a few participants, but the anticipated number is roughly targeted and can allow for some flexibility.

SUGGESTED AGE RANGE

Designated ages may seem oddly specific in some cases, but we are drawing on experience to indicate who may get the most out of a particular event. This book is designed to target programs to four different age categories, but the variations offered in each section will help you get the most out of library program resources and time.

SHOPPING LIST

The program descriptions are designed for you to use as blueprints, including lists of specific supplies. Items in the list do not always need purchasing, such as a laptop and projector. The shopping list is meant to ensure that everything essential to run that program is at hand.

SETUP

Activities listed in this section specify marketing tips (sometimes months ahead), time spent contacting speakers in some cases, and room setup the day of the event. Shopping time is not listed, but should be assumed necessary for each event.

MAKE IT HAPPEN

Specific actions required on the day of the event are listed in this section.

VARIATIONS

Look at this section for ways to make programs appeal to different ages or for ways to take the topic covered to online media for virtual participation.

POWER PROMOTION

Marketing the Oscar Night program may be very different from marketing the Microwave Magic and Easy-Bake Oven Adventures program. This section gives tips on subject-inspired marketing where applicable. Simpler versions of the individual events could be used for the monthly clubs. For example, the Smart Tips for Self-Publishing program in December would appeal to members of the Writers' Workshop, and some of the self-publishing information could be distilled into a handout or a brief discussion for the club members. Another way to market programs that cross the interest levels of different age groups is to schedule them directly after a club meeting. Members could stay for the event, which could draw in more people as well. Yet another way to cross-market is to advertise the program instead of the club meeting that month. The program can be expanded to fill more time than the usual meeting, and members can be encouraged to attend along with other interested patrons.

CLUBS

After the individual programs have been introduced, we offer an additional chapter on clubs. The clubs can be used in a few different ways. The activities in that chapter are grouped by theme and are designed to fill shorter monthly or recurring meetings. The ideas listed for each club are not designed by themselves to fill a stand-alone program. However, some of the activities could be combined to make larger events or to gauge interest in a topic for a possible club. For example, suggested topics for meetings of the Writers' Workshop include queries, contests, and the business of writing. Those topics could easily fill a 60- to 90-minute, one-night information program for interested patrons. Additionally, many of the stand-alone programs from the monthly chapters can be adapted for use as shorter programs for the clubs.

Few programs run the same way twice in public libraries, and knowing the needs and desires of patrons in the community may change how programs are handled. This book is meant as a guide to inspire.

JANUARY

FITNESS AND HEALTH goals are a great way to start off the New Year! Plan a simple Fit Fair to introduce patrons to community health services and classes. It will also remind everyone that the library is the place to try exercise DVDs or learn new, healthy recipes.

Help ward off cabin fever with Old-School Gaming. Older teens and people in their 20s may discover games that the 30- and 40-year-olds grew up enjoying. Adults looking for quiet activities will enjoy talking about books while eating themed foods with Great Reads and Treats for Book Clubs. For a fun family library program, consider a variation for moms with tots or for parents and children.

Families are created in different ways today, but the choices and processes can be daunting. Help your local families learn about alternative ways to expand their families at an Adoption and Foster Care program in the comfort of the library.

Adults armed with new resolutions, gadgets, and spirit will be heading into the library for guidance and entertainment.

FIT FAIR

Offer patrons a chance to sign up for interactive demonstrations or just drop in and get information about fitness trends and opportunities at this fun event.

PREPARATION TIME	LENGTH OF PROGRAM	NUMBER OF PATRONS	SUGGESTED AGE RANGE
2 hours	4 hours	25 for demonstrations, unlimited for stations	30s–40s

SHOPPING LIST

- » Yogurt
- » Fruit
- » Raisins
- » Bowls
- » Spoons
- » Raffle items (such as refillable water bottles, pedometers)

SETUP

3 to 6 Months Before

- » Contact staff at local grocery stores, park districts, fitness centers, and martial arts studios about doing brief demonstrations on healthy eating and exercising at the fair.
- » Consider having two interactive demonstrations with patron registration specified by age range in between other scheduled events for the fair. Patrons in their 30s and 40s may not want to exercise among older teen patrons and may have different strength-training exercises targeted to their needs.
- » Agencies may want to send a representative and put out materials about classes rather than offer a class, and patrons will enjoy that, too.

1 Week Before

- » Pull video games, DVDs, and books on healthy eating and exercising to be used at the fair. Test video games ahead of time to be sure all components are working.
- » Call outside speakers for demonstrations to confirm setup needs.

1 Hour Before

» Set up equipment for video gaming or DVD stations. Set out fruit and other healthy snacks.
» Set up a table for each agency involved in the fair, including a table for library materials. The tables may be separate from the room in which the demonstrations or classes are held so that patrons may continue to browse materials throughout the program, even if they are not attending a demonstration or class.

MAKE IT HAPPEN

» For the healthy snacks, consider offering patrons plain or low-sugar yogurt to mix with toppings such as fruit and raisins.
» Invite adult patrons to try some of the exercise video games or sport games, such as Zumba Fitness for Wii or Your Shape for Xbox. If the games require patrons to register or get a body assessment, be sure the stations are not attached to an easily viewed screen for privacy.
» Run exercise DVDs throughout the event.
» Invite patrons to guess how many steps it takes to get from the farthest spot in the library's parking lot to the program. Offer a prize for the correct answer.

VARIATIONS

» Online: To build interest in the fair, feature fitness gadgets such as Fitbit on library social media sites. Ask patrons what gadgets they have and what tips they can offer for using them. Feature each agency offering a demonstration on the sites as well.
» Fit for Fines: Inspire patrons throughout January to clear fines by dropping off a healthy snack recipe or exercise tip throughout the month. Forms should be available online or on bookmarks placed in reserved items. Recipes can then be featured on social media sites.
» Older Teens: Exercise video games will appeal to older teens. Consider a smoothie or yogurt parfait–making program with video game stations for teens to drop in and enjoy.

POWER PROMOTION

All agencies involved in the event will want to promote it at their facilities. Be sure to offer signs, flyers, or brochures for all interested agencies.

OLD-SCHOOL GAMING

With at-home game systems becoming popular in the 1970s and taking hold more and more throughout the ensuing decades, adults in their 20s, 30s, and 40s were the first generations to grow up with video games. An old-school gaming program is a great way for participants to engage in nostalgia as well as socialize with like-minded peers.

PREPARATION TIME	LENGTH OF PROGRAM	NUMBER OF PATRONS	SUGGESTED AGE RANGE
1–2 hours of setup	2–3 hours	25	20s–40s

SHOPPING LIST

Ideally, this program can largely be achieved with what your library already has on hand. Although your library might have a substantial number of video games, the crux of this program is the "old-school" factor. It is not likely that your library will have "vintage" (relatively speaking) video games on hand, so if you're going to focus mostly on video gaming, consider marketing the program as a "Bring Your Own Game/System" event. Encourage participants to bring their old-school video games and game systems from home, while you provide the space and televisions necessary to play.

SETUP

2 Months Before
» Take inventory of what equipment you have at your disposal—how many TVs, extension cords, and gaming systems you have on hand.

1 Week Before
» Come up with a plan to gather all of the electronic equipment that you'll need for the program, as well as how you're going to move it all into the program space.

2 Hours Before
» Move equipment into your program space. Plug everything in and test it to make sure it all works. Gather whatever games you have on hand, and make sure you take note of their titles, barcodes (if applicable), and conditions so that you'll know what you should be collecting at the end of the program.

MAKE IT HAPPEN

» If you are going to incorporate video gaming into your program, you will need a substantial amount of electronics. Holding the program in a large room with plenty of electrical outlet access will be key. Depending on the setup of your library, you may also have to move several televisions into one room.

VARIATIONS

» Board Games: The old-school factor of this program can also be achieved with board games, which tend to be easier to acquire en masse and require substantially fewer (basically no) power sources or electronic elements. Classic board games such as Monopoly, Life, and Trivial Pursuit are always favorites, but keep in mind that these games can run quite long. Other classics such as Sorry!, Trouble, Connect 4, and Yahtzee can make for great tournament games if your patrons are up for it.

POWER PROMOTION

» Place flyers and posters near your library's video game collection as well as near other popular browsing locations, such as DVDs and music.
» Visit local game stores and comic shops and ask to post flyers advertising the program in those establishments.

GREAT READS AND TREATS FOR BOOK CLUBS

One of the staples of readers' advisory programming is a book club. Kick-start or reinvigorate a traditional library book club by pairing exciting books or genres with tasty treats found at the grocery store or bakery or, if desired, made at the library. Who doesn't want to share their opinions about books they have loved or loathed while eating delicious snacks?

PREPARATION TIME	LENGTH OF PROGRAM	NUMBER OF PATRONS	SUGGESTED AGE RANGE
2–3 hours for shopping and setup	1 hour	25	20s–40s

SHOPPING LIST

- » Microwavable plates
- » Cups
- » Bottled water
- » Plastic or permanent silverware
- » Snacks or treats
- » Napkins
- » Book

SUGGESTED PAIRINGS

COUNTRY AND BOOKS	TREAT
France » *Anna and the French Kiss* by Stephanie Perkins » *Let Them Eat Cake* by Sandra Byrd » *Chocolat* by Joanne Harris	Chocolate fondue with pretzels, marshmallows, and a selection of fruits: bananas, strawberries, pineapple, kiwi, apples
Ireland » *P.S. I Love You* by Cecilia Ahern » *Angela's Ashes* by Frank McCourt	Irish soda bread, Green River soda
Scotland » *Outlander* by Diana Gabaldon » *Girl Meets Boy* by Ali Smith	Shortbread, samples of whiskey, cranachan
England » *Death Comes to Pemberley* by P. D. James » *Austenland* by Shannon Hale	Scones and clotted cream, selection of teas
Japan » *Battle Royale* by Koushun Takami	Wasabi peas, sushi, various candies: Pocky, Lychee, Jelly

SUGGESTED PAIRINGS (continued)

GENRE AND BOOKS	TREAT
Thrillers and Killers Book Club » *Gone Girl* by Gillian Flynn » *Still Missing* by Chevy Stevens » *I'd Know You Anywhere* by Laura Lippman	Death by chocolate (cake)
Not Quite Grown-Up Reads » "New Adult" Fiction » *Beautiful Disaster* by Jamie McGuire » *Graduates in Wonderland* by Jessica Pan and Rachel Kapelke-Dale (nonfiction) » *Fangirl* by Rainbow Rowell	Junk food and wine pairings or sparkling grape juice in plastic flutes with fancy chocolates
Nonfiction, Humor » *I Like You* by Amy Sedaris » *Yes Please* by Amy Poehler	Cheese pâté with pineapple (retro)
Sweet Reads » *The Peculiar Sadness of Lemon Cake* by Aimee Bender » *Pies and Prejudice (A Charmed Pie Shoppe Mystery)* by Ellery Adams	Lemon cake, bars, or pie
American History » *Mrs. Lincoln's Dressmaker* by Jennifer Chiaverini » *The Wedding Dress* by Virginia Ellis » *Persian Pickle Club* by Sandra Dallas	Apple pie

SETUP

2 Months Before

» Decide what book and treat you want to use for your book club. Read the book and buy extra copies to loan to patrons in the upcoming months. Put together a shopping list for supplies.

1 Week Before

» Prepare ten to fifteen discussion questions for the program. *Helpful Hint*: Publishers often have discussion questions online or at the ends of books.
» Go shopping for supplies or order baked goods from a bakery or grocery store if necessary.

1 Hour Before

» Arrange the tables in your program room into a square to allow all participants to see one another and to facilitate discussion.
» Arrange the treats decoratively on a table along with the paper supplies.

MAKE IT HAPPEN

» Greet patrons as they enter the room and encourage them to grab a tasty snack.
» Proceed to ask the discussion questions and get opinions about the story and characters. Include a question about other possible treats from the story that participants would have enjoyed.

VARIATIONS

» Older Teens: Plan a quarterly book club with one main young adult book and treats that revolve around the chosen book. Have the teens create and decorate the treats with a logo or cover similar to the main character or book cover.

POWER PROMOTION

» Create bookmarks that advertise the event along with a picture of the treat(s) that will be served. Place these in circulating copies of the books for patrons who might be reading the book but not know about the event.
» Create a poster that advertises the book and treat pairing and ask to hang it up at the bakery or grocery store you are partnering with in your community.
» Put out a themed display in the weeks leading up to the event and be sure to include flyers advertising the event.

POWER PARENTING
ADOPTION AND FOSTER CARE

Families interested in pursuing infertility treatments, adoption, or foster care often do not know where to begin their process. These topics are personal and scary. The process of adding a child to the home can be expensive and stressful. Free, informational programs at the library allow potential parents to learn more easily. This topic could cover a series of workshops, including a panel on the experiences of adopted children and teens, international adoptions, special needs adoptions, and preparing the house for foster or adoption certification.

PREPARATION TIME	LENGTH OF PROGRAM	NUMBER OF PATRONS	SUGGESTED AGE RANGE
1 hour	90 minutes per topic	50	30s–40s

SHOPPING LIST

» Index cards
» Pencils

SETUP

2 Months Before
» Contact any local adoption agencies and foster care centers to inquire if staff would be willing to be on a panel about the processes involved. Ask if it would be possible to have a panel of families with children, teens, or both. Library staff with adopted families may be willing to participate in a panel as well. With enough interest from possible speakers, determine if more than one topic could be covered. The program could be split into two topics, such as domestic and international adoption, or adoption and foster care.
» Make sure that flyers are available throughout the community (see the Power Promotion section) and that the program or series is advertised on social media.

1 Week Before
» Confirm all setup needs with speakers. If families, children, or teens will be participating in a panel, consider providing a small thank-you gift for each speaker.
» Make a list of library materials about adoption and foster care to give to attendees.

1 Hour Before

» Set up and test all audiovisual equipment.
» Make sure that information on all agencies represented is listed on a handout and placed on the seats along with paper and pencils.
» Hand out question cards to patrons as they come in. Collect the cards throughout the program and give them to the panel to answer. Audience members may not feel comfortable asking personal questions.

MAKE IT HAPPEN

» As audience members come in, encourage them to fill out question cards when they sit down.
» Introduce speakers.
» Facilitate with question cards.

VARIATIONS

» Networking: Adoptive families or foster care families often enjoy networking. Consider hosting a quarterly get-together by theme to introduce families to the library and offer a fun craft activity or movie.
» Holiday Happening: Kwanzaa and Chinese New Year are times when mixed families want to learn about traditional cultural practices, and the library could host programs for those events.

POWER PROMOTION

This event really needs word-of-mouth promotion to locate the folks looking for this information. Putting flyers at local religious organizations, in hospitals or doctors' buildings, throughout the library, and at fitness centers in the area will likely find the target group.

FEBRUARY

RETAIL STORES MAY be looking ahead to spring, but in many areas, patrons are still shoveling snow and piling on layers of clothes. Programs this month bring patrons into celebrations of food and fun to offer relief from the throes of winter.

Not everyone loves Valentine's Day, but an Un-Valentine's Day can be much more appealing for those not feeling the love. From fancy to just plain fun, a library Oscar Night can celebrate the best in a year of films in a variety of interactive, enjoyable ways.

Kick off the spring season Mardi Gras–style with a memorable themed evening complete with masks and plastic babies. Finally, rather than follow a theme, a basic DIY café drinks demonstration at the Hot Drink Mixology event offers delicious tips on how to indulge without expensive and fancy drink makers.

UN-VALENTINE'S DAY

Valentine's Day is a polarizing holiday, and it provides a wealth of programming options. In fact, celebrating a disdain for Valentine's Day can be even more entertaining than a traditional Valentine's Day program. Anti-Valentine's Day parties are nothing new, and they present a great opportunity for fun library programming that incorporates crafting, playing games, and watching movies.

PREPARATION TIME	LENGTH OF PROGRAM	NUMBER OF PATRONS	SUGGESTED AGE RANGE
3 hours shopping and setup	1½ hours	25	20s–30s

SHOPPING LIST

- » Red, heart-shaped piñata
- » Large bags of candy
- » Blindfold
- » Foam bat

- » Blank greeting cards
- » Markers
- » Stencils
- » Prepackaged heart-shaped sugar cookies

- » Decorating frostings with tips
- » Napkins
- » Paper plates

SETUP

2 Months Before
- » Decide what crafts and treats you want at the program and create a shopping list. Also, think about incorporating music as background entertainment and put together a playlist.

1 Week Before
- » Shop for supplies—except for sugar cookies, which should be purchased the day of the program.

1 Hour Before
- » Gather supplies into the program area and set up stations for each craft option.

MAKE IT HAPPEN

» Set up different stations for each craft or treat.
» Un-Valentine Making: Provide blank greeting cards, markers, and stencils to be used for creating the perfect opposite-of-valentines.
» Cookie Decorating: As a play on hearts with sweet sayings, put out the heart-shaped cookies and decorating frostings and encourage participants to come up with their own creative sayings.
» Pick a time during the program at which you will gather everyone to participate in the smashing of the piñata. Randomly assign numbers as guests show up and draw the numbers to decide who gets to go first. Like we did when we were kids, blindfold each participant and spin him or her around a couple of times before allowing the chance to swing.
» If you want to include a game in the program, consider the always-popular Apples to Apples. Although it doesn't have an explicit anti-love theme, it provides abundant opportunities for funny and even crass combinations and is a great way to get a group of patrons who might not all know each other to laugh together.

VARIATIONS

» Show a Movie: Consider showing a movie that participants can watch while they craft or just watch if they so choose. For something lighthearted, you could go with *The Break-Up*, or if you feel like being dangerous, there's *My Bloody Valentine* or *Fatal Attraction*. Keep in mind that you'll need to adjust your projected program length to accommodate the length of the movie.

POWER PROMOTION

If your library has a romance section, consider posting flyers for the program there. Also consider posting them near movie and music collections in your AV department.

OSCAR NIGHT

Offer some Oscar night viewing or a glamorous tribute to past winners at this fun event for movie lovers.

PREPARATION TIME	LENGTH OF PROGRAM	NUMBER OF PATRONS	SUGGESTED AGE RANGE
3 hours	3 hours (much shorter than the actual ceremony)	50	20s–30s

SHOPPING LIST

- » Sparkling grape juice
- » Plastic champagne glasses

- » Trophy statues for trivia games (replicas of Oscar)
- » Red plastic runner for floor

- » Popcorn
- » Other snacks as desired
- » Napkins
- » Pencils

SETUP

2 Months Before
- » If the library is not open on Sunday nights, consider offering the program after hours for Oscar viewing.
- » If an after-hours event is not possible, invite patrons to vote either on print ballots or online for which of several recent years' winners or the current year's contenders that they would like to see.
- » The winning movie can then be shown at a designated event during library hours. As patrons register, they could be encouraged to vote at that time, too.

1 Week Before
- » Design some Oscar night trivia about past winners, famous costume missteps, host gaffes, and more. A few trivia questions or contests could take place throughout the program.
- » Brochure copy should indicate that anyone wearing fancy dress will be entered in a special raffle for a statue.

1 Hour Before
- » Set down the runner for the red carpet.
- » Set out bowls of popcorn and glasses of the grape juice "champagne."
- » Be sure the AV equipment is working.

MAKE IT HAPPEN

- » As people arrive, take their picture and ask them about their favorite movie before they sit down with snacks and prepare to watch the movie or the Oscar broadcast.
- » Before the movie or Oscar broadcast, warm up the crowd with some trivia questions or show opening monologues from a few past hosts, available on YouTube. Take an informal poll about who has seen the contending movies and who will win awards. Hand out the big trivia game and pencils.
- » Offer intermission during the movie to award prizes for the trivia winners.
- » At the end of the movie or broadcast, draw a name from those who came in fancy dress and award another statue.

VARIATIONS

- » Oscar Live Texting: Invite patrons to take photos and post with an Oscars hashtag throughout the program, from the library account. This could be set up on an iPad and handed around or left in an easily accessible place during the program.
- » Oscar All Day Long: Show past winners in a program open to all ages throughout the day of the Oscar event or in preceding days.
- » Oscar Viewing Program: Beginning January 1, invite patrons to record which current or previous Oscar contenders they watch throughout the month. Patrons who view five or more would be eligible for a prize, such as a bag of gourmet popcorn, in similar fashion to reading programs. Invite patrons to offer short reviews and log their activity online through the Events software (http://evancedsolutions.com) or Facebook groups. This program can help build interest for the movie-viewing event.

POWER PROMOTION

- » Patrons visiting the AV area may be most interested in this event, so post flyers in this area.
- » Displays with statues and previous Oscar movies will attract attention.
- » Removable stickers with program information on DVDs in the display may help advertise.

MARDI GRAS

Those outside Louisiana and nearby areas of the South may know little about Mardi Gras and how it is celebrated. Bring Cajun-style fun to your community with the flavors, music, and style of the famous celebration.

PREPARATION TIME	LENGTH OF PROGRAM	NUMBER OF PATRONS	SUGGESTED AGE RANGE
2 hours shopping and setup	1½ hours	25	Older Teens

SHOPPING LIST

- » Toy crowns (2–3)
- » King cake with plastic baby (coffee cake with a purchased plastic baby also works)
- » Sparkling grape juice
- » Praline candies
- » MoonPies (http://moonpie.com)
- » Plastic beads
- » Hurricane mix or seltzer water (mixes can be found online or at big-box stores)
- » Plastic cups
- » Paper plates
- » Napkins
- » Powdered-sugar doughnut holes (in place of beignets)
- » Plain masks
- » Embellishments like feathers, rhinestones
- » Permanent markers
- » Craft glue
- » Cards for BINGO using MARDI instead (make a new heading strip and tape it onto purchased cards or use a free online bingo card–making site). Gold coins could be place markers if space allows, or use colored M&Ms in green, purple, and gold.

SETUP

1 Month Before
- » Order masks, MoonPies, and Hurricane mix if not available locally.
- » Check with local bakeries to see if one can make a king cake or large coffee cakes for the party.
- » Purchase plastic babies to put in each cake or to have a spare (some people like to keep theirs).

1 Week Before

» Pull zydeco and jazz music from the library collection or use online stores if necessary. Play the music at times in the AV or teen areas and mention the program to patrons to drum up interest.

» Make a display of books and movies set in New Orleans, incorporating beads and a few masks.

» Make up some New Orleans and Mardi Gras trivia questions, such as, What are some things thrown from floats? (Answer: beads, MoonPies, candy, etc.)

1 Hour Before

» Set out treats and supplies for activities.

MAKE IT HAPPEN

» As older teens arrive, play music and give each a string of beads to wear.

» Slice the king cake and pass out pieces. One piece should have the plastic baby inside. Whoever gets that piece is the "king" and gets to wear the crown.

» Invite everyone to decorate masks.

» Pass out MARDI cards and place markers while waiting for the glue on the masks to dry. Winners could also receive crowns.

VARIATIONS

» Mardi Gras Movie: Patrons in their 20s and 30s could also enjoy this event and may enjoy watching *The Big Easy* or other movies set in New Orleans in addition to other activities.

» Family Mardi Gras: Patrons in their 40s may enjoy a family Mardi Gras program—a streamlined version of the Older Teen event.

POWER PROMOTION

» Staff could wear beads in the days before the event to advertise, or masks the day of the event.

» Play zydeco and jazz music from the library collection in the AV or teen areas.

HOT DRINK MIXOLOGY

With the price of a hot coffee averaging between $4 and $6, you can help your patrons save money by learning how to brew their own beverages. Although it would be easiest to do this with an espresso machine, it is possible to use a regular coffee machine or similar product. Offer a variety of hot coffees, chocolates, syrups, and flavors. Allow patrons to experiment, discover new combinations, and learn how to re-create popular favorites.

PREPARATION TIME	LENGTH OF PROGRAM	NUMBER OF PATRONS	SUGGESTED AGE RANGE
2 hours	1 hour	15–25	20s–40s

SHOPPING LIST

- » Microwave
- » Espresso machine, AeroPress espresso machine, or a French press
- » Paper cups
- » Wide, shallow coffee cups

- » Permanent marker
- » Napkins
- » Plastic spoons
- » Coffee
- » Flavored syrups (variety)
- » Marshmallows
- » Hot cocoa

- » Peppermint sticks
- » Cinnamon sticks
- » Jar with lid
- » Milk (2% or nonfat)
- » Sugar
- » Half-and-half

SETUP

2 Months Before
- » Ask if anyone on staff has an espresso machine you can borrow for the program. If not, purchase one online or at a store (they are fairly inexpensive).
- » Consider the setup of the room, additional supplies, and what types of drinks you would like to make: lattes, cappuccinos, macchiatos, hot cocoa, tea, and the like.

1 Week Before
- » Create a shopping list and purchase supplies.
- » Test the instructions and make a handout with instructions for the types of drinks you can make.

1 Hour Before
- » Set up different stations: cups, drinks, microwave, flavors, and garnishes.
- » Start to brew coffee and wait for patrons to arrive.

MAKE IT HAPPEN

» Have people label their cups with a permanent marker.
» Give a tutorial on the two coffees being brewed and how they're different. For example, a latte is made with espresso, steamed milk, and milk foam. A cappuccino is similar, but has a greater percentage of foamed milk than steamed milk.
» Use the Espresso machine or substitute to make coffee. Fill the wide, shallow cups about one-third to one-half full depending on how strong you like coffee.
» Pour milk into the jar until it's half full, cover, and shake vigorously for 1 minute. Uncover and microwave for 30 seconds.
» Pour the steamed milk into the coffee (the portion amount will depend on the type of drink) and spoon the foam onto the top of the drink.
» Encourage patrons to experiment with the various drinks and flavors.
» Vote on favorite combinations and see if anyone figured out how to make his or her favorite designer drink.

VARIATIONS

» Cider Mixology: Experiment with different cider combinations and spiced drinks. Make different spice mixes to take home and enjoy on a crisp autumn day.
» Older Teens: Taste test different brands and flavors of hot cocoa. Do a blind test and see if fancy hot chocolate is any better than generic store brands. Allow teens to do mix-ins of flavored syrups.
» Craft and Snack: Offer a fall crafts and snacks class. Teens can enjoy apple cider and apples while they create a fall-themed craft such as leaf painting or making autumn leaf bowls.

POWER PROMOTION

» Post flyers at train stations and gyms where people congregate during early hours.
» Pass out mini samples of coffee at the train station on an early morning to entice others to join. Have flyers or be ready to sign up people remotely.

MARCH

SPRING INTO MARCH with a blend of celebration, change, and lots of green things!

Combine sports-style competition and reading with March Madness, complete with tournament-style brackets and levels. Craft Brewing night will help those who are interested in the increasingly popular hobby start or learn tips to enhance their beverages. The beer doesn't have to be green just because the program is in March.

The St. Patrick's Day or Green Party will combine a fun event with an environmentally friendly, or green, project. Get your growing on with the Seed Bomb and Terrarium DIY and enjoy some crafts with plants for indoor projects, too. The Social Justice and Activism program offers a way for patrons to learn about and get involved in important causes.

Interactive events from this month will help inspire new passions for adult patrons.

MARCH MADNESS

It's not difficult to get people interested in this annual event, and putting a library spin on it is a great way to spice up those months between winter and summer reading programs. There are tons of options when designing this program to fit the needs of your library community—and it can be as complicated or as simple as you want to make it, so choose whatever works best for you!

PREPARATION TIME	NUMBER OF PATRONS	SUGGESTED AGE RANGE
Allow several hours for creating the brackets as well as setting up the online voting component.	Unlimited	Older Teens and 20s–40s

LENGTH OF PROGRAM

When we first came up with this idea, we envisioned it lasting throughout the month of March. Bracket pickup and the making of predictions should happen during the last week of February so that voting can begin on March 1. Depending on how many matchups you choose to go with, you'll want to space out the voting evenly so that participants have time to cast their votes.

SETUP

2 Months Before
» Determine the theme for your contest (1980s movies versus 1990s movies; contemporary book characters versus classic characters, etc.), and fill out the initial thirty-two matches.
» Determine by what means voting will take place (library website, Facebook, etc.).
» Decide what the exact start date of the contest will be, which will determine when patrons will need to have their brackets filled out and handed in.

1 Week Before
» Have blank brackets for patrons to fill out ready to be distributed at public service desks.

MAKE IT HAPPEN

» Though it is not absolutely necessary, consider having a kickoff event at which patrons can fill out and turn in their brackets as well as enjoy some refreshments and general celebration. If you decide to forgo a kickoff program, make sure that patrons know where to pick up brackets to fill out well in advance of the start of voting.

» Start with sixteen slots on either side of the bracket (or fewer if you want to have a quicker contest), making a total of thirty-two initial entries on the form. The idea is to pick a theme for each side of the bracket—for example, characters from classical literature (sixteen) on one side and characters from contemporary literature (sixteen) on the other side.

» Patrons will be able to pick up a bracket and fill it out according to their own preferences or predictions. Completed brackets must be turned in before March 1, when voting will begin.

» Winners of each bracket will be determined by patron votes. Voting will take place by weeks. In other words, all of the voting for round one matches will take place during the first week of March. Patrons will have the entire week to cast their votes for the first sixteen matches. Voting for round two will occur during the second week of March, and so on. An official bracket will reflect the winners of each poll.

» Winners of each matchup will be determined by voting. Depending on your technological means, you can create weekly polls on social media or on your library's website imploring visitors to vote for their picks. Because voting will last only a day or so for each matchup, paper voting is not feasible.

» Points will be awarded for picking the correct winner of each pairing, and the number of points for each correct selection will increase by round (correct pairings for round one, for example, can each be worth five points; round two, ten points, etc.). The final winners will be determined by the number of points earned by each person.

» Prizes can be given however you choose. One choice is to award one grand prize to the person who earns the most points overall. Other prizes can be given to those who correctly predict the ultimate winner.

VARIATIONS

» Age Group Brackets: This program has potential appeal across all patron age groups, so different brackets can be set up for different ages—perhaps one in the children's department, one in the teen/young adult department, and one in the adult department.

» Streamlined Brackets: As mentioned, you can start with fewer brackets if the task of creating and maintaining so many polls is daunting.

CRAFT BREWING

Craft brewing is an increasingly popular hobby among adults of all ages, especially males. This is a great opportunity to help re-brand the library's image as a vibrant learning environment that values the interests of a younger demographic.

This program is best done in two sessions: one for preparing the beer and the other two weeks later for bottling the beer. The beer must ferment in the fermentation buckets for ten to fourteen days before bottling. Make sure you have access to a stove and an area to store your fermenting beer.

PREPARATION TIME	LENGTH OF PROGRAM	NUMBER OF PATRONS	SUGGESTED AGE RANGE
2 hours for setup and shopping	4 hours (divided into two sessions— 2 hours per session)	10–20	21–40s

SHOPPING LIST

» Brewing starter kit
» Pale ale brewing kit
» Large stock pot (5 gallons)
» Bleach or sanitizer
» Glass bottles
» Caps

SETUP

2 Months Before
» Seek out home brewing experts or craft beer store personnel and ask them to do a presentation about craft brewing at the library. Ask what beer is the most popular and easiest to brew.
» Ask presenters to bring their own equipment. If presenters do not provide the equipment, see the preceding shopping list and buy online.
» Check with your local government agency to see if a liquor license is necessary to brew beer or taste it.

1 Week Before
» Confirm with the presenters and ask about equipment and technology needs.

1 Hour Before
» Set up tables and sanitize the equipment as directed in the instruction kits.

MAKE IT HAPPEN: SESSION I

» Prepare beer as directed in the home brewing kit (add water, malt extract, hops, etc.).
» While the brew is cooling, ask the presenters to talk about the science behind brewing, equipment, popular beers, and trends in the brewing world.
» Stir in yeast vigorously and seal the bucket for fermentation.
» Let the brew ferment for 10–14 days.

MAKE IT HAPPEN: SESSION II

» Transfer beer from the fermentation bucket to the bottling bucket.
» Make the sugar solution to add to the bottling bucket. Add and stir well.
» At this point, the beer is ready for tasting. If your patrons want to taste it, they can if your library allows it or you have a liquor license.
» Bottle the beer. Fill and cap the bottles. The beer will be ready to drink in 10–14 days.

This is a simple form of home brewing. Some home brewing kits may vary or the presenters may choose a different recipe. Follow the instructions of the presenters or the kit.

VARIATIONS

» Sample Time: Visit a local home brewing store and have a beer sampling class or tour. Or ask local craft brewers to bring their samples to the library for a tasting.
» Beer and Barbecue: Pair a beer tasting and barbecue class. Make it a tailgating event in the library parking lot.
» Older Teens: Create various smoothies out of fruits and mixes. Taste test and determine the best combination. Pair this with a yoga or healthy eating program.

POWER PROMOTION

» This program will require a lot of outside promotion. Post flyers at train stations, gyms, and bars.
» Ask your presenters to advertise the program at their home brewing or craft beer stores.

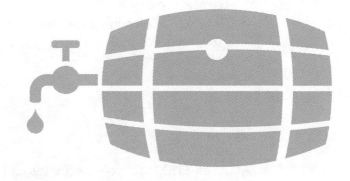

GREEN PARTY

Invite patrons to wear green and be green at this enjoyable event. Beyond themed activities, attendees will also work on projects to help their community. Several activities are listed here, and any could be eliminated to save time or resources.

PREPARATION TIME	LENGTH OF PROGRAM	NUMBER OF PATRONS	SUGGESTED AGE RANGE
3 hours shopping and setup	1½–2 hours	25	Older Teens

SHOPPING LIST

» Rain barrel for library or local community garden: look for inexpensive plastic drums at bottling companies or online. Rain barrels can cost $50. A searchable directory of local sources for recycled plastic drums and barrels can be found at http://gardenwatersaver.com/containers/.
» Plain, small flowerpots
» Appropriate paints for surface of rain barrel and pots
» Light sandpaper up to 220 grit for preparing the surface of barrel. Useful information on preparing the plastic rain barrel for painting can be found at www.ehow.com/how_6725469_paint-plastic-barrels.html.
» Clear sealant for after the rain barrel is decorated
» Brushes
» Sponges
» Dirt

» Seeds (extra packets may be purchased for prizes)
» Baggies
» Plain cupcakes or small cookies to decorate
» Green frosting, if available, otherwise dyed vanilla frosting
» Sprinkles
» Green fruits: apples, pears, grapes
» Green River soda or green juice
» Small, plain tote bags
» Sharpie permanent markers
» Table and floor coverings for projects
» Paper plates
» Napkins
» Fimo clay
» Toaster oven (a used or thrift store one that will not be used again for food is best)
» Foil (to wrap trays in toaster oven while baking clay charms)
» Keychain fixings (available at craft stores)
» T-pins
» Wire cutters

Optional
» BINGO game
» Green M&Ms for tokens (extras can be used for cupcake or cookie decorating)

SETUP

2 Months Before
» Source the rain barrel, plants, tote bags, and paints. Order and purchase as much as possible.
» Ask staff if anyone has an old toaster oven to donate, or contact local thrift stores.

1 Week Before
» Prepare the rain barrel for painting and put on one coat of paint.
» Contact local bakeries or grocery stores to order plain cupcakes. Large cookies would work if cupcakes are not available.
» Shop for cupcake decorating supplies, Fimo clay, keychain materials, planting soil, seeds for flowers (for individual pots), and permanent markers in several colors.

1 Day Before
» Shop for cupcakes or cookies, fruit, and drinks.
» Put the dirt into individual baggies for participants. It is best to do this outside.

1 Hour Before
» Set up the room with copious table coverings. It may be best to paint the rain barrel outside or, if that's not feasible, in the garage of the library. If painting must be done indoors, be sure to cover the floor and open the windows.
» Separate out the green M&Ms, if desired, for BINGO.

MAKE IT HAPPEN

Painting Pots and Rain Barrel
» This needs to be done first to allow time to dry. Ask the group if they would like a theme for the rain barrel.
» At the Schaumburg Township District Library, the teens elected to do a starry night and sky theme. A few people can be working on the rain barrel at a time while the others are painting their individual pots with brushes.
» After the program, the rain barrel will need a coat of sealant within the next week before it can be donated and put into use at the library or at a local community garden.

Lucky Charms
» Attendees should then work on the Fimo clay charms for their keychains. Charms should not be bigger than about ¾" square.
» When charms are finished, pierce each piece with a T-pin, removing the pin before baking, so a small hole is left.
» Charms must be baked for 25 minutes, which may require two shifts of baking.
» After the charms are baked, put a T-pin through each charm and affix it to the keychain ring or hardware.

Cupcake Decorating and Snacks
» Participants will decorate cupcakes (or cookies) and snack on the other green foods.

Tote Bags
» Another environmentally friendly project is decorating tote bags with the Sharpies.

BINGO
» It is good to have this game on hand in case the drying and baking take more time. Prizes for this activity could be seed packets.

All participants should receive a baggie of planting soil along with seeds, a tote bag, and a keychain.

VARIATIONS

» Rain Barrels Expanded: Individual recycled rain barrels can be decorated, which may be better as an outdoor event. Rain barrels can also be auctioned or raffled to benefit a local food pantry, community garden, or the library.
» For 20s–30s: These groups will enjoy many of these activities as a St. Patrick's Day Party.

POWER PROMOTION

» Samples of any of the projects in a display of St. Patrick's Day materials will attract attention.
» Irish music played in the AV or teen areas will also remind patrons of the event.
» If a local community garden will be receiving the donation of the rain barrel, the city, township, or village halls may also be interested in advertising the event.

SEED BOMB AND TERRARIUM DIY

A great way to put on a green celebration for your emerging adult patrons is with this hip take on a gardening program. Seed bombing involves tossing small bundles of soil and seeds into areas that are lacking in flora in an effort to promote biodiversity. The seed bomb portion of this program will entail the creation of the seed bombs and a presentation by an authority on the practice. That is coupled with a workshop on creating and caring for one's own terrarium.

PREPARATION TIME	LENGTH OF PROGRAM	SUGGESTED AGE RANGE
1 hour (plus additional time to find and hire presenters)	2½ hours	20s–30s

NUMBER OF PATRONS

15–20 (or more, depending on the comfort level of the person[s] leading your workshop[s])

SHOPPING LIST

TBD depending on what the presenter(s) will provide

SETUP

4–5 Months Before

» Find presenter(s) for your program. Before you jump to hiring someone to come in and lead a terrarium workshop, ask around among your colleagues and see if anyone happens to have a terrarium hobby.

» If you are unable to find an instructor internally, there is a chance that someone who has put on a similarly themed program at your library also does terrarium construction and would be willing to teach the workshop.

» As for seed bombing, kits and instructions can be found online, but we recommend having someone who is familiar with the principles of seed bombing speak at and lead the program.

2–3 Months Before

» Work with your presenter(s) to determine what supplies they will provide and which ones you will be expected to purchase for the program, if any.

1 Week Before

» Purchase supplies, if necessary.

1 Hour Before

» Set up presenters' stations (see the Make It Happen section for details) as well as tables and chairs for participants.

MAKE IT HAPPEN

» If your program space allows it, set up separate stations for each portion of the program. You'll need tables and chairs for your participants to sit at and use as work spaces, as well as tables for your presenters to use for their demonstrations.
» A good plan might be to form two groups of participants (depending on how many you have), with one group starting at the terrarium DIY and one starting at seed bombs. After both groups have completed the presentation at their respective stations, have them switch places.

VARIATIONS

» Single Event Program: It is obviously not necessary to do this program with both the seed bombing and the terrarium DIY elements. If you think one or the other is more feasible given your patron base and geographic location (for example, seed bombing has caught on especially in urban areas), then go with what you are most comfortable with as well as what works best with your budget.
» Seed Exchange: If you don't think seed bombing will be a hit in your area, you could substitute a traditional seed exchange, in which participants bring seeds from their own gardens to trade with one another. This option requires less preparation and is easier on your budget.

POWER PROMOTION

Create a book display of your library's gardening and terrarium construction manuals and include informational materials about your program(s).

SOCIAL JUSTICE AND ACTIVISM

Give people an opportunity to become active contributors and make a difference in their community by responding to issues bigger than themselves. Whether it is on a local, national, or international level, everyone deserves to be treated equally regardless of his or her race, gender, or sexual preference. The library can help promote human rights and shed light on issues that are affecting the world and your community. These concerns can range from human trafficking, veterans' rights, and environmental conservation to racism, sexual assault, bullying, and more. Find a cause that you are passionate about and involved in and speak about ways to get involved, or invite counselors or advocates from organizations.

PREPARATION TIME	LENGTH OF PROGRAM	NUMBER OF PATRONS	SUGGESTED AGE RANGE
2 hours	1 hour	20–30	20s–40s

SHOPPING LIST

- » Presentation system
- » Computer
- » Pens
- » Paper
- » Coffee
- » Water bottles

SETUP

2 Months Before
- » Choose which cause you would like to speak about and advocate for.
- » Begin researching the issue, important organizations, laws, and different ways to get involved.
- » Contact local human rights groups, legal aid advocate lawyers, government officials, or crisis centers to ask for information and advice or to invite them to speak.

1 Week Before
- » Create a handout for participants with important websites, books, and organizations to help find information about the issue.
- » On the other side of the handout, include contact information for government officials to whom participants can send letters, e-mails, or petitions requesting changes in policies, and information about where local volunteer centers are located.

1 Hour Before

» Pull books from the collection that pertain to the issue and have them available for checkout.

» Make coffee for participants.

MAKE IT HAPPEN

» When people arrive, have them sign in and write down what other causes or interests they would like to learn more about.

» Conduct the presentation or moderate the panel.

» What is the issue? Who does it affect? How many people does it affect each day? Each month? Each year?

» Include information about nonprofits, government agencies, and groups fighting against your cause.

» What laws are currently in place and what potential laws are on the agenda in the near future?

» How do people get involved? Discuss different time commitments and how people can help. Options include volunteering to train as a counselor, attending a rally, working a hotline, sending letters to or calling government officials about a policy, and more.

» What can the library do to help this cause? Offer resources, books for people of all ages, the opportunity for open discussion, and a chance to make a difference.

VARIATIONS

» Many times the need for and response to a specific program is very timely. Examples include the ALS Ice Bucket Challenge, September 11, or the Sandy Hook Elementary School shooting. For events such as these, try to incorporate an activity into another program the library is hosting or create a separate program and promote it via social media. One example of such a response is Snowflakes for Sandy Hook Elementary School after the tragic shooting in December 2012. Teachers asked people to create paper snowflakes to decorate the halls of the school. After September 11, some libraries hosted memorial services and candlelight vigils.

» Speak about the current events that are affecting our world. Timeliness is often key for activism programs, and programs may have to be pulled together quickly in response to an event.

» Invite an author who has written about a specific issue or supports a specific cause to speak at the library or in a video chat. Pair this speaker with a charity or organization that supports the same cause.

» Volunteers in Action: Some people may be inspired to do more than learn about these issues, volunteer once a week, or donate money. Programs such as Teach for America, AmeriCorps, and the Peace Corps train people to be full-time volunteers. Ask representatives to speak at a presentation or volunteer fair.

» Online: Video chat with a Peace Corps volunteer overseas. Have him or her talk about life overseas and experiences in the Peace Corps.

POWER PROMOTION

» The United Nations designated February 20 as World Day of Social Justice. Schedule your program close to this day or frame the program around the day.

» Create a display with other informational books that highlight the issue.

» Ask the organizations involved and other nonprofits in the area to post flyers and spread the word about the event.

» Work with the library's Volunteer or Service Club (see the Clubs That Keep Them Coming Back chapter) to collaborate on a project, memorial service, or campaign for a cause of the members' choice.

APRIL

CLEANING, COLLECTING, AND creating are celebrated this month with inspiring programs for adults.

Poetry Month can be enjoyed by both creators and audience members with a night of reading, or patrons can travel back in time to '80s Night for themed fun.

Help patrons recycle while they make money. The Spring Cleaning Sale takes recycling to a profitable level for patrons, and Curating Collectibles helps patrons know what to do with treasures. First-time home buyers can find smart strategies at the Money Smart Week program.

POETRY READING NIGHT

Hosting a night of poetry is a great way to creatively engage your community and promote literacy. Provide a forum for a night of poetry readings and encourage aspiring poets to share original work to reach a broader demographic and audience. This is a great way to bring together poetry fans and enthusiasts as well as poets. Have small, cutout, card stock note cards available for people to create poems to take home or post at the library if they are shy about sharing in front of a group.

PREPARATION TIME	LENGTH OF PROGRAM	NUMBER OF PATRONS	SUGGESTED AGE RANGE
1 hour setup	1–2 hours	10–50	20s–40s

SHOPPING LIST

- » Fruit trays
- » Cookies
- » Paper plates
- » Plastic forks
- » Napkins
- » Card stock
- » Calligraphy or stylistic pens

SETUP

2 Months Before
- » Secure a room in the library. Even the lobby or a reading room would be advantageous to reach a wide audience.
- » Invite a local drum group that will allow people to use the drums to create a vibrant energy in the room.
- » Collect old typewriters from the library or staff members for participants to use to create poetry on the spot.

1 Week Before
- » Gather poetry books and print out poems by popular poets. Make sure to include poems and authors who are unknown or local.
- » Make a shopping list for supplies and purchase everything that is nonperishable.

1 Hour Before
- » Arrange chairs in an amphitheater setting with a microphone and speaker (optional) and the drums behind them.
- » Set up two tables—one with the appetizers and the other with typewriters, card stock, and calligraphy pens for people to create poems.

MAKE IT HAPPEN

» Start the night off by thanking participants for being brave enough to share their own poetry, and inspire others by sharing your own poem.
» Encourage participants to read their original works, but be prepared to have readings of better-known poems.
» Ask participants to make extra-crafty typewriter and calligraphy poems and hang them in the lobby or a reading room of the library.

VARIATIONS

» Reach out to a local museum or performing arts center that will partner with the library for a night of poetry and creativity for adults. Encourage formal wear and serve appetizers.
» Older Teens: Have a slam poetry contest in which teens compete based on their performance and poetry. Provide different drums or acoustic instruments that they have to use in their piece.
» Blackout Poetry: Create blackout poetry with discarded library books. Scavenge through weeded books and use them to create a poetry craft. Have participants black out and emphasize specific words with Sharpie markers to create powerful pieces of poetry with specific words on a page. Encourage doodling and high-lighting to create unique works of art that enhance the poems.

POWER PROMOTION

» Host the poetry event in April to coincide with National Poetry Month.
» Post flyers at local coffee shops and distribute to writers' groups.
» Display famous lines of poetry in your flyer and proclaim, "Your poetry could be next!"

'80s NIGHT

Chances are a decent portion of your emerging adult patrons came of age in the decade of John Hughes movies, Garbage Pail Kids, and Members Only jackets. And who doesn't want to jump in a time machine and enjoy all of the best treats, games, and music that the 1980s gave us?

PREPARATION TIME	LENGTH OF PROGRAM	NUMBER OF PATRONS	SUGGESTED AGE RANGE
3 hours shopping and setup	2 hours	30	20s–40s

SHOPPING LIST

» '80s candy assortment (Airheads, candy necklaces, Nerds, Lemonheads, Milk Duds, Now & Laters, Reese's Pieces, and the like)
» Board games
» Card stock in neon colors
» Markers
» Large cardboard box, flattened

SETUP

2 Months Before
» Create a shopping and supply list based on what elements you've chosen to include in your program.
» Depending on what '80s board games and snacks you want to have at the program, you might need to start looking for them sooner rather than later.
» Thrift stores are a good place to check for retro board games.

1 Week Before
» Shop for supplies and gather items that can be found, not purchased (for example, a large cardboard box that you will flatten and use for break dancing).

1 Hour Before
» Set up various gaming, crafting, and snack stations.
» Cue up a movie or playlist if you're going to incorporate either one into the program.

MAKE IT HAPPEN

Game Table
» Connect 4, Trouble, Battleship, Rubik's Cubes, Dream Date, and so on.

Corner of Room
» Twister

Crafts Table
» Fortune Tellers
  1. Cut the neon card stock into 8½" × 8½" squares.
  2. Fold a square diagonally each way, making sure to create a crease at each fold.
  3. Fold the piece of paper in half each way, once again creating a crease at each fold.
  4. Fold each corner in toward the center, creasing each fold.
  5. Flip the paper over and, again, fold the corners in toward the center.
  6. Fold the paper in half, and slide your fingers under the pockets that have been created to give the fortune teller its shape.
  7. Set out markers so that participants can come up with their own creative options for their fortune tellers.

» Place a large square of cardboard on the floor—probably in one corner of the room—for break dancing. Invite participants to bust a move!

» Consider having a playlist of awesome '80s music playing throughout the program. Check your library's music collection for soundtracks from popular '80s movies as well as other '80s compilations.

VARIATIONS

» There's a bounty of totally rad '80s movies that you could show during the program (see Retro Movie Night in the Clubs That Keep Them Coming Back chapter for inspiration). If you don't want to detract from the other goings-on during the program, you could have the movie playing in the background (as opposed to a playlist). That way, participants can dip in and out of the movie as they see fit. You can also have impromptu movie-oke showdowns among your participants!

» Consider holding a best-dressed competition and award prizes to participants who are wearing the best '80s costumes. (Make sure to advertise this competition in all of your program promotions so that attendees know to dress up!)

» You can also hold an abbreviated '80s trivia competition highlighting the movies, music, TV shows, and important events of the decade (see Trivia Nights in the Clubs That Keep Them Coming Back chapter for inspiration).

» See the Retro Craft Club in the Clubs That Keep Them Coming Back chapter for more fun craft ideas!

POWER PROMOTION

» Post flyers near your browsing AV collections such as CDs and DVDs. If possible, create a display of '80s music and movies and include on the display information about your program.

» Reach out to local comic shops and game stores and ask to post flyers in their establishments.

SPRING CLEANING SALE

Invite patrons to host their own tables or bring items for a spring cleaning swap or flea market. These can have a theme, such as toys, books, or holiday decorating items.

PREPARATION TIME	LENGTH OF PROGRAM	NUMBER OF PATRONS	SUGGESTED AGE RANGE
2 hours	3 hours	15–20 patrons hosting tables, event open to public	20s–40s

SHOPPING LIST

No supplies are needed for this event. It is helpful to have cash and change available on the day of the event.

SETUP

2 Months Before
» Make up application forms for patrons who desire to host a table for the event. On each form, ask for contact information, the name(s) of the patron(s) who will be manning the table, and what items will be sold.
» On the form, indicate the dimensions of the table.
» List any rules about the sale: types of items that may or may not be sold and whether items may be placed next to or underneath the table. Remind patrons that the library is not responsible for stolen or damaged items.
» If a percentage of the sales is going to a charitable cause, make that clear.
» Assign tables in order of receipt of applications. For example, tables closest to the door are in possibly the best spot and should be assigned to those who turn in their forms first.

1 Week Before
» Remind participants of their setup time. If they will be unloading at a back entrance, provide instructions on how to do that. Let patrons begin unloading and setting up well before the program start time.
» Remind patrons that items must have prices clearly marked and that table hosts should provide their own change at each table. At the Schaumburg Township District Library, table hosts placed a unique, assigned letter on each item. Items were rung up at a central table run by library staff, with some staff keeping track of what was sold for which letter. Money was cashed out and given to hosts at the end of the event. This works well especially if staff members want to host tables.

» Invite teen volunteers to help with unloading before the event and packing up afterward.
» Pull items from the library book sale area to offer at the event if possible.
» Invite staff to donate used plastic bags for attendees to use for any items they sell or purchase.

2 Hours Before
» Be sure plenty of carts are available to help people who are bringing items to the sale.
» Tables with a couple of chairs each should be in the designated sale area, either a meeting room or the lobby of the library.

MAKE IT HAPPEN

» As table hosts arrive, volunteers should help them unload and get their items to their table.
» When the event begins, circulate to ensure that things are going smoothly. Ask for feedback from table hosts about what is working well, what is selling best, and how the event can be improved in the future.
» At the end of the program, volunteers should help table hosts pack up and load their vehicles.
» If a portion of sales is going to a charitable cause or to the library, this can be handled in different ways. A small registration fee can be collected with the application from each person who wants to host a table. Or staff can ask each host for a donation at the end of the day. The cause can also be advertised, with a collection jar, near the entrance of the event.

VARIATIONS

» Swap and Save: No money would change hands at this version of the event. To encourage people to host tables, offer hosts 30 minutes to shop and swap among themselves before the public is allowed. The swap may be most easily handled by using a theme such as craft supplies and kits, music and books, toys, kitchen items, or holiday decorations.
» Library Clean Out: Library staff can offer leftover craft supplies, prizes from older reading programs, and more at a table during library book sales or at a table during the Spring Cleaning Sale or the Swap and Save event.
» Appraising Event: Invite someone from a local antiques mall or thrift shop to give estimates on people's portable treasures. Another option is to have library staff use a laptop and some reference books to help people discover the current market value of their items. Advertise that estimates can change and that people may each bring in one easily carried item.

POWER PROMOTION

» Distribute prewritten copy advertising the event to all table hosts and encourage them to put it on their social media.

» Put bookmarks with information about the event in book sale items in libraries that run a continuous book sale.

CURATING COLLECTIBLES

Some people collect antique lamps. Some people collect stamps. Some people collect McDonald's Happy Meal toys. No matter what a person collects, even if she or he is just getting started, learning how to catalog, organize, and display a prized collection can be helpful and fun.

PREPARATION TIME	LENGTH OF PROGRAM	NUMBER OF PATRONS	SUGGESTED AGE RANGE
1 hour (plus additional time to find and hire presenters)	1½ hours	25	20s–40s

SHOPPING LIST

» 3" × 5" note cards

» Pens

SETUP

2–3 Months Before

» Ask among your staff to find out if any are collectors. Keep in mind that the point of your program is to provide information, so you'll want to choose people for the panel who are serious collectors and feel comfortable talking about what they collect, as well as details about how they collect and display items.

» Once you've exhausted your resources within the library, reach out to local toy stores and collectibles shops (such as sports memorabilia and music) and find out if they have people on staff or know of people in the community who would be willing to participate on the panel.

1 Week Before

» Compile some questions that you'd like to ask the panel so that you're prepared in case your audience isn't as participatory as you would like. General questions to consider asking are these:
   – What sorts of guidelines do you set for yourself as a collector?
   – Do you also sell your collectibles, and, if so, what means do you use?
   – Are you part of collecting groups or forums online?
   – What advice do you have for people who are wondering what their collections at home are worth?
   – What advice do you have for people who are just getting started collecting?
   – Do you catalog or keep some kind of manifest for your collection? If so, what program do you use and what is your process?

1 Hour Before

» Set up tables (enough to seat all of your presenters) at the front of your presentation space, with chairs in the audience facing them.
» Place note cards and pens near the entrance to your presentation space.

MAKE IT HAPPEN

» As participants enter the room, point out the table where you have placed the note cards and pens and encourage them to write down any questions that they have. The panel moderator then has a place to start when the program gets under way. Let your participants know that if they don't have any questions right away that is fine, as there will be opportunities to ask additional questions throughout the panel discussion.
» When the program starts, allow each presenter to introduce himself or herself and give a brief summary of his or her experiences with collecting. Proceed with the questions you have prepared in advance as well as those that have been submitted by the audience.
» Encourage your presenters to bring pieces or pictures of their collections to share with the audience. If possible, create a PowerPoint display that you can project throughout the program that includes these pictures.
» Note: Make it clear in your promotional materials for the program that the presenters are not there to appraise anyone's personal collections.

VARIATIONS

» Although it is not the purpose of this program to have participants bring items for appraisal, you could consider having an *Antiques Roadshow*–esque program in which that is the focus. Offering appraisals will require reaching out to local antiques dealers and collectors to find someone who is competent enough to appraise the myriad items that patrons could bring in.

POWER PROMOTION

» If professionals from your community are participating on your panel, ask them if they are willing to plug the program on their social media and in their shops (if applicable).
» Create a display of books about collecting and antiquing and place on it information about your program.
» If your library has closed display cases, create a display of various "collectible" materials (old toys, lunchboxes, comic books, stamps, etc.—see what your colleagues will be willing to briefly donate) and include with it information about the program.

MONEY SMART WEEK
FIRST-TIME HOME BUYERS

Money Smart Week is a public awareness campaign designed to help consumers better manage their personal finances, often through library programs and community partnerships during one week every April (see www.moneysmartweek.org). Although traditionally many programs have been organized for children, teens, and established adults to learn about managing their finances, very few topics and opportunities are targeted at helping emerging adults learn about financial subjects important to them. This is an excellent opportunity to engage emerging adults by spotlighting their unique needs, including first-time home ownership.

PREPARATION TIME	NUMBER OF PATRONS	SUGGESTED AGE RANGE
2 hours for setup and shopping	25–50	20s–30s

LENGTH OF PROGRAM

1½ hours: 45 minutes for panel presentation, 15 minutes for questions, 30 minutes for individual or private questions.

SHOPPING LIST

» Bottled water
» Light refreshments
» Homeowner and DIY home repair materials (for giving away or checking out)

SETUP

2 Months Before
» Coordinate with your business or community liaison librarian and reach out to bankers and real estate agents in your community. Ask them if they would be willing to speak at a panel presentation about becoming a first-time homeowner. Assemble a panel of experts from the community that would cover different topics. For example, bankers might discuss the requirements for a loan application, different types of loans, mortgages, and finance rates. Real estate agents could discuss what buyers should look for in a house, how much buyers should spend in relation to their income, and typical pitfalls or traps to avoid. Seek these experts' advice about what they feel would be the most helpful to potential owners.

2 Weeks Before

» Confirm with your presenters and ask them if they have any technology needs. Create a list of FAQs and handy tips for first-time buyers; don't be afraid to ask your sources. Match these with available library materials or online resources.

» Order home repair books to give away and stamp them with your library's logo in preparation for patrons' new journey into home ownership. Begin publicity by targeting grocery stores, local community colleges, banks, real estate agents' offices, train stations, and gyms.

1 Hour Before

» Set up a table for the guest speakers and any required technology, including a microphone.

» Offer water or light refreshments to speakers.

MAKE IT HAPPEN

» Greet patrons as they enter and engage them in conversations about where they are in the home buying process. Remind them of the library's resources and ask them how the library can help them.

» Act as a moderator and keep the panel focused. As a non-financial expert, you have a somewhat limited role in this program.

» Allow time at the end of the presentation for questions and provide one-on-one time for people to speak privately about sensitive information.

» By assembling a panel of experts, you are providing the opportunity for patrons to learn how to embark on a new phase of their life. This is also an excellent opportunity to network and work with businesses in your community.

VARIATIONS

» Older Teens and Parents: Many teenagers have little to no experience with basic budgeting or credit cards. Offer a workshop about what it takes to get a credit card, the different types of credit cards available, APRs, and hidden fees.

» First-Time Renters: For the adults who are not quite ready for the commitment of a home but are still daunted by the prospect of moving out on their own, offer a first-time renter's program.

» Investing with a Little: Host an investment workshop for those who are just beginning their adult lives but may not have the secure finances of an established individual who has been saving for years.

POWER PROMOTION

» Create posters and flyers for banks, community colleges, real estate offices, currency exchange centers, or loan offices.

» Place ads on popular real estate or credit loan websites.

» Create handouts or inserts for credit and loan books in a Money Smart Week display.

MAY

TRAVEL THROUGH TIME and around the world with programs during May. Help your patrons plan vacations that involve Road Tripping across North America from Canada to Mexico, learn how to travel to Europe on the Cheap, or head back a few decades with '90s Night food and activities.

Finish out the month by offering a Memorial Day Service Fair featuring volunteer opportunities for adults in the community.

FROM CANADA TO MEXICO
ROAD TRIPPING ACROSS NORTH AMERICA

The sprawling continent of North America is a cultural jackpot of diversity. Canada, Mexico, and the United States offer a wealth of activities for all interests: sports, city life, history, culture, adventure—all within reach by car. Some may think taking a road trip is just a simple act of jumping in the car and hitting the road, but when traveling hundreds or thousands of miles, it is worth the effort to prepare ahead of time.

PREPARATION TIME	LENGTH OF PROGRAM	NUMBER OF PATRONS	SUGGESTED AGE RANGE
3 hours	1 hour	15–30	20s–40s

SHOPPING LIST

- » Licorice
- » Trail mix
- » Chips
- » Soda and bottled water
- » Napkins
- » Paper plates
- » Map
- » Thumbtacks
- » Scissors
- » String
- » Computer
- » Presentation system

SETUP

2 Months Before
- » Begin researching attractions and activities in Mexico, Canada, and the United States.
- » Prepare a presentation featuring some of the different types of activities in these countries: where they are located, what they cost, and what ages they are appropriate for.

1 Week Before
- » Buy road trip snacks: licorice, trail mix, chips, soda, and bottled water.
- » Create a road trip checklist to help patrons stay safe on the road: fluid levels, tire pressure, jumper cables, a phone charger, a GPS or map, and the like.

1 Hour Before
- » Set up tables and snacks for patrons to enjoy.
- » Tape a map onto a tackboard or a wall and place thumbtacks, scissors, and string nearby.

» Pull audiobooks and encourage patrons to check them out. Set up the computer and presentation system.

MAKE IT HAPPEN

» Greet people as they enter and encourage them to eat a typical road trip snack. Ask them to use the thumbtacks and string to trace their road trip route and stops along the way.
» Road Trip Checklist: Show patrons how to check fluid levels and tire pressure. Remind them to pack jumper cables, a phone charger, and a GPS or map.
» Crossing the Border: Discuss documents and identification travelers will need to cross the borders. Go over restrictions on food, weapons, and animals.
» Canadian Highlights: Niagara Falls, Whistler for skiing enthusiasts, Avonlea (the setting for *Anne of Green Gables*) for literature buffs, Vancouver Island, the city of Toronto. (These and the following two lists are just a few of our own ideas; they are a small sample of all the great things North America has to offer.)
» Mexican Destinations: Archaeological ruins and landmarks (Tulum, Guadalajara, Merida), Los Cabos for water sports fans, and Oaxaca, which has one of the best festivals celebrating Día de Los Muertos (Day of the Dead).
» Touring the USA: Divide the country into regions and feature interesting attractions for each area: in the South, Civil War battlefields and plantations; on the East Coast, Washington, D.C.; in the Midwest, Chicago's numerous museums or the Willis (formerly Sears) Tower; and in the West, Yellowstone National Park in Montana or the world-famous San Diego Zoo in California.
» How can we help you? Share resources the library has available to make road tripping safe, affordable, and a once-in-a-lifetime experience.

VARIATIONS

» Great American Campout: Are patrons intrigued by the idea of camping, but don't know where to start? Share the dos and don'ts of camping, discuss what supplies are necessary, offer recipes for fun meals to cook over a fire, and in general help patrons find out what to expect.
» Day of the Dead: Invite patrons to learn about the historical and cultural significance of Día de Los Muertos. Decorate sugar skulls and create a Day of the Dead craft.

POWER PROMOTION

» Create an audiobooks display to help road trip fans pass the time. Advertise the program on this display and insert flyers into the audiobooks.
» Give out car air fresheners with the library logo and information promoting this program.
» Make a display featuring books for North American travel and auto repair. Feature this program prominently with the display.

EUROPE ON THE CHEAP

Traveling is an exciting but nerve-wracking prospect that may intimidate many first-time or less experienced travelers, especially when going overseas to a foreign country. Although many people know to use travel websites to book airline tickets, they may not know the road less taken or ideas that will save them both time and money. Take the worry and fear out of traveling abroad by hosting a night of cheap travel tips for adults.

PREPARATION TIME	LENGTH OF PROGRAM	NUMBER OF PATRONS	SUGGESTED AGE RANGE
3 hours	1 hour	15–30	20s–30s

SHOPPING LIST

» Snacks from different countries
» Napkins
» Paper plates
» Map
» Pushpins or dot stickers
» Computer
» Presentation system

SETUP

2 Months Before

» Begin to research and create an online resource page of favorite websites to use to find the best deals for airfare, housing, and transportation.
» If you or other staff members are familiar with overseas traveling, put together a presentation about cheap ways to travel in Europe.
» Another option is to ask a travel agent or travel writer to speak and offer advice.
» Break down the presentation by transportation, attractions, and cultural connections or by country.

1 Week Before

» Create a handout of free activities and attractions in popular cities.
» Include handy travel tips and a checklist of important items: passport, alarm clock or watch, universal power adapter, photocopy of passport, phone numbers for the country's U.S. embassy, and the like.
» Print a budgeting worksheet for people to fill out at home.
» Shop for international treats a few days before the event: check out the Great Reads and Treats for Book Clubs program in the January chapter for snack ideas.

1 Hour Before

» Set up tables and snacks for patrons to enjoy.
» Tape a map onto a tackboard or a wall and have pushpins or stickers available next to it.

MAKE IT HAPPEN

» Greet people as they enter and encourage them to eat an international treat. Ask them to put a pushpin or sticker on the map to mark future travel destinations.
» Accommodations and transportation: Discuss the different options available in Europe and how they differ from traveling in the United States—for example, budget airlines, the Eurail pass, trains, buses, and ferries. Budget hotels, hostels, and couch surfing are all cheap housing options.
» Attractions: Give ideas for cheap or free activities and tourist attractions. For example, city or museum passes offer dozens of tourist attractions for a one-time fee. Many literary and historical sites are free, such as the Somme battlefield in France, the Berlin Wall, and cafés where famous authors penned best sellers. To see the inside of a famous church, travelers may attend services. The natural world is almost always free—patrons can explore the Alps or the beaches of Spain.
» Money Traps: Raise patrons' awareness of hidden international fees on credit cards, hotel cancellation charges, and touristy restaurants—many of these have higher markups and charges.
» Cultural Connections: Offer advice on social and cultural norms of different countries. For example, if travelers ask for water, they will be served mineral water and charged accordingly. Savvy travelers ask for tap water instead.
» Budgeting: Encourage patrons to create a budget and stick with it! Pass out a budgeting worksheet for people to take home to get started on the trip of their dreams.
» Offer to research specific countries and interests for participants. Sit down one-on-one or in a group and discuss a specific country or type of activity they might be interested in. E-mail ideas and suggestions to individuals or the group.

VARIATIONS

» Backpacking Overseas: One of the great rites of passage is backpacking through Europe. Show patrons how to plan, pack, and survive with only the clothes on their backs.
» Country-Specific Travel on the Cheap: Tailor this program to a single country overseas. Discuss specific attractions, cultural norms, and transportation options to make traveling easier.

POWER PROMOTION

» Make an online ad or web banner for the library's online language learning databases. If someone is learning a new language, he or she may also be interested in traveling to a new country.
» Create a display of nonfiction European travel books, language learning books, or audiobooks and feature the program.
» If you are ordering program snacks from a bakery or grocery store, ask to hang flyers promoting the program.

'90s NIGHT

As with the '80s party (see the April chapter), this is a great opportunity to relive some iconic elements of a decade in which many of your patrons grew up.

PREPARATION TIME	LENGTH OF PROGRAM	NUMBER OF PATRONS	SUGGESTED AGE RANGE
3 hours shopping and setup	2 hours	30	20s–40s

SHOPPING LIST

- » Chocolate pudding snack cups
- » Oreos (original)
- » Gummy worms
- » Plastic spoons
- » Paper plates
- » Napkins

- » '90s candy and snack assortment (Baby Bottle Pops, SweeTarts, Caramel Apple Pops, Warheads, Fruit by the Foot, Gushers, Fruit Roll-Ups, Capri Sun)

- » Embroidery floss in a variety of colors (especially neon)
- » Scissors
- » Karaoke machine

SETUP

2 Months Before
- » Create a shopping and supply list based on what elements you've chosen to include in your program.

1 Week Before
- » Shop for supplies and gather items that can be found, not purchased (check with staff members to see if anyone is willing to loan you some LEGOs. Go for the generic sets as opposed to the themed ones to avoid mix-ups and lost pieces).

1 Hour Before
- » Set up various gaming, crafting, and snack stations.
- » Cue up a movie or playlist if you're going to incorporate either one into the program.

MAKE IT HAPPEN

» DIY Snacks: Have a station where participants can make their own dirt cups using the pudding snack cups, gummy worms, and crumbled Oreos.
» Set up an additional table for candy and snacks.
» Karaoke Corner: Set up the karaoke machine in one corner with plenty of space for brave individuals to show off their skills (if you're planning to incorporate this activity in your program, keep in mind how it will affect your playlist or movie-showing options).
» Craft Table—Friendship Bracelets: Set up a table with embroidery floss and scissors so that participants can re-create the magic of making friendship bracelets. Check your library's holdings for friendship bracelet–making instruction books to place at the table.
» LEGO Table: If you can get your hands on some LEGO sets, set up a table or two for your participants to construct to their hearts' content.
» Consider having a playlist of awesome '90s music playing through the program. Check your library's music collection for soundtracks from popular '90s movies as well as other '90s compilations.

VARIATIONS

» Costume Contest: Consider holding a best-dressed competition and award prizes to participants who wear the best '90s costumes. (Make sure to advertise this competition in all of your program promotions so that attendees know to dress up!)
» Trivia Contest: You can also hold an abbreviated '90s trivia competition highlighting the movies, music, TV shows, and important events of the decade (see the Trivia Nights Club in the Clubs That Keep Them Coming Back chapter for inspiration).
» Consider showing a classic '90s movie during the program (see the Retro Movie Night Club in the Clubs That Keep Them Coming Back chapter for inspiration). If you don't want to detract from the other goings-on during the program, you can have it play in the background (as opposed to a playlist); that way, participants can dip in and out of the movie as they see fit. You can also have impromptu movie-oke showdowns among your participants!
» See the Retro Craft Club in the Clubs That Keep Them Coming Back chapter for more fun craft ideas!

POWER PROMOTION

» Post flyers near your browsing AV collections such as CDs and DVDs.
» If possible, create a display of '90s music and movies and include on the display information about your program.
» Reach out to local comic shops and game stores and ask to post flyers in those establishments.

MEMORIAL DAY SERVICE FAIR

Lots of young adults looking for their first job or ways to help out in their community do not know how to get experience helping. Busy nonprofit organizations do not always have enough help, but they also do not have the time and resources to train volunteers. A volunteering fair can help both groups. Adding a food or clothing drive or library volunteer training to the event may bring in more people.

PREPARATION TIME	LENGTH OF PROGRAM	NUMBER OF PATRONS	SUGGESTED AGE RANGE
2 hours	2 hours	Unlimited	Older Teens–20s

SHOPPING LIST

No supplies are necessary. Giving the host organization cookies or drinks is a nice, but optional, touch.

SETUP

3–6 Months Before
» Contact local nonprofit agencies to discover which ones would be willing to host a table soliciting volunteers. If organizations are unable to provide people, offer tables for placing materials and volunteer sign-up sheets. Suggest also that some of the organizations' volunteers may be willing to sit at tables and answer potential volunteers' questions.
» Solicit library staff to discover what volunteering needs the library may have and see if staff are willing to take groups on tours and do basic training during the program. Registration can be taken for those interested in volunteering at the library for a designated period during the fair. Current library volunteers may be interested in leading tours or in helping at the event as well.

1 Week Before
» Double-check all details with members of the other agencies as well as library staff interested in helping to recruit and train volunteers at the event.

1 Hour Before
» Be sure the room is set up.
» Make a central sign-up or evaluation sheet for participants with an option for an e-mail address at which they can be contacted by all participating agencies.

MAKE IT HAPPEN

» Encourage participants to visit each table and fill out an evaluation form.
» Those who bring in food or clothing for a specific drive for a community group can be entered in a raffle to win a fine-free coupon.
» Have staff or volunteers take small groups of the potential library volunteers on tours as they arrive, including staff locations. When the tour is over, basic and brief training on sorting or other common tasks can fill the rest of the designated time and give staff a chance to get to know the potential volunteers better.
» After the event, give community group staff members a chance to evaluate the program also, either informally in conversation or by filling out a form.

VARIATIONS

» Lobby Displays: Throughout a week or during weekends in May, members of community groups could host a table or take sign-ups for volunteering from all age groups. Collecting materials or food for drives would be a visible and attention-getting way to keep momentum going.
» Online: Feature a few local groups with volunteer needs each week throughout May on a designated area of the library website or social media outlets.

POWER PROMOTION

» Provide posters, signs, or flyers to each community group involved, along with brochure copy sent in e-mail to promote the program to their clients.

6

JUNE

HERE COMES SUMMER!

Help patrons make the most of June events and celebrations. Offer fun and inexpensive ideas with a series of DIY Wedding and Shower Accessories programs featuring everything from headpieces and hairstyles to favors. Share tips on local foods by letting your audience know how and where to shop for delicious and fresh items at the Farmers' Market Fair.

Celebrate June traditions. LGBT Pride Month can be supported by the library in several interactive ways. Or save yourself time and energy when attracting adults with Realistic Summer Reading and Media programs. Broken down by target ages for adults, these suggestions will help staff find tips and ways to make the programs more workable for these time-pressed groups.

Head into the busy season for public library staff with summer-friendly programs and strategies.

DIY WEDDING AND SHOWER ACCESSORIES

Everyone planning a wedding or shower is looking for ways to cut costs while celebrating in style. Help brides by offering an all-day program or a series of programs designed to help them add their own touches to their events. Many of these topics can also be useful for longer programs held at different times of the year; for example, the hair and headpiece topic would be great in April for prom planning.

PREPARATION TIME	NUMBER OF PATRONS	SUGGESTED AGE RANGE
4 hours shopping and setup	40 per session or topic	20+ (young women may want to bring mom or grandma)

LENGTH OF PROGRAM

Four 1- to 1½-hour programs with a different, advertised topic for each program or an all-day event with different topics at different times for 4 hours total.

SHOPPING LIST

Supplies will vary per topic and requirements of speakers. Suggestions are included in the Make It Happen section.

SETUP

3–6 Months Before
» Although staff may be able to offer demonstrations on some of the topics outlined, professionals may also be willing to offer demonstrations in exchange for advertising their businesses. It is likely that speakers will need to be paid for their time or at least for their supplies.
» For the hair and headpiece topics, invite a hairdresser from a local salon to provide demonstrations or a presentation with photos.
» A local craft store representative may be willing to discuss DIY headpieces and basic cupcake decorating.
» Contact a florist about offering a demonstration on basic DIY centerpieces.

» Invite a staff member from the computer department or graphics area to show basic computer photo card manipulation and card design options as well as different card design software.
» See if any staff members in the library can offer a short demonstration on any of the topics. Many people have been through wedding planning and have great time- or money-saving ideas.
» Contact local bridal shops and ask them to advertise the event with flyers or signs.

1 Week Before
» If the speakers require supplies, be sure everything is readily available.
» Double-check with all speakers to ensure they have all of their needs for their part of the events. For example, cupcakes, frosting, and tools may be needed for the cake decorating session so that patrons can try some of the techniques.
» Shop for supplies for any topics that staff will be demonstrating.

1 Hour Before
» Before each session, check the room setup and AV equipment.

MAKE IT HAPPEN

» As people come in, give them a handout with information about each topic and the date or time of that session.
» Hair and Headpieces: Introduce the speaker, review upcoming sessions and topics, and assist as needed.
» Photos and Computer Cards: This topic will be covered in 45 minutes with the cupcake decorating taking up the remaining 45 minutes. The speaker from the library computer or graphic design staff can show some software best for photo editing, papers good for printing photos, and some simple save-the-date or shower invitation cards that could be done on the computer.
» Cupcake Decorating for Beginners: If the craft store representative or cake decorator (from a bakery if the craft store person is not available) is able to offer this as an interactive workshop, hand out cupcakes, plates, frosting, simple decorations, and tools. If not, circulate with samples so everyone can see the designs being demonstrated.
» Flowers: A florist will demonstrate some DIY alternatives to centerpieces or corsages and boutonnieres for weddings and showers using fresh or dried flowers.
» Favors and Wedding Touches: This session could be conducted by staff beginning with a slideshow of practical favor ideas found online. These could include photo frames, dish towels or simple utensils tied in ribbon, tea or coffee packets, bags of mints or heart-shaped chocolates, and more. A few of these ideas could be demonstrated.

» Recipe Scrapbook: For this session, show attendees how to put together a recipe scrapbook for the bride. Patrons can gather recipes of their own or ask friends and family members of the bride for copies of favorite recipes. Inexpensive, plastic, flip photo albums can hold all the recipes. These scrapbooks could be done on a theme such as family recipes, quick and easy dinners, or delicious desserts.

» Sachets and Mints: Show patrons how easy it can be to take precut circles of netting, add some potpourri or mints, and tie with thin ribbon in a variety of colors to create these always popular favors.

» Ring Bearer's Pillow and Garters: Again, slides of ideas can be shown or demonstrated with simple sewing or gluing techniques. One popular technique for making a ring bearer's pillow involves weaving ribbons and fusing them down onto fusible interfacing before sewing the pillowcase, turning it right side out, and decorating with rings and colored ribbons in the center.

VARIATIONS

» Offer parts of these topics in one session or have a DIY fair with professionals and crafters doing demonstrations at tables. Patrons can walk through, see techniques, and get information.

» Online: Make short videos on some of these topics with local professionals offering tips on how brides can save time and money—for example, by making their own favors or invitations. As an option, feature each topic with links to how-to articles and YouTube videos.

POWER PROMOTION

» Provide signs and flyers for each professional outlet involved in the event.

» Display library media on these topics along with samples or a running slide show to garner further attention.

FARMERS' MARKET FAIR

Farmers' markets help bridge the gap between the country and the city and suburbs by providing fresh fruits and vegetables in a mutually rewarding exchange. They are of great value to communities and encourage people to shop locally. At this program, invite local farmers who participate in farmers' markets to bring in samples of their produce and talk about their farm, crops, shopping locally, a specific crop's outlook, their experiences in the farmers' market, and so on. This is a great opportunity for individuals and families to personally meet the people who grow their food and learn the process behind how food comes to their tables.

PREPARATION TIME	LENGTH OF PROGRAM	NUMBER OF PATRONS	SUGGESTED AGE RANGE
2 hours	2 hours	20–40	20s–40s

SHOPPING LIST

- » Paper plates
- » Napkins
- » Knife
- » Toothpicks

SETUP

2 Months Before
- » Contact local farmers' markets and ask individuals or the organization to participate in the fair. Farmers' markets are organized and managed in a variety of ways—by farmers' groups, local governments, or community groups.
- » Ask farmers, market managers, or organizations to provide demonstrations and to share any knowledge about agriculture or farmers' markets.

1 Week Before
- » Confirm that the farmers and other presenters will be able to attend.
- » Create name cards with each farmer's or presenter's name, farm location if appropriate, and the market where the individual sells his or her produce.

1 Hour Before
- » Move tables into a half circle around the room with chairs for the presenters.
- » Place the name cards on the tables where the presenters will sit.
- » Make sure all of the produce being sampled is washed.

MAKE IT HAPPEN

» Greet people at the door and encourage them to talk to different farmers about their produce and markets where they sell.
» Have farmers talk about the projected crop outlook for the upcoming months. Find out what vegetables and fruits are best in specific seasons.
» Ask for a demonstration about how to tell if certain types of fruit are ripe and how to cut them properly (for example, pineapple, cantaloupe, mango, etc.).

VARIATIONS

» Online: Plot different local farmers' markets on a map and indicate the dates and times they are open. Ask patrons to help identify new ones and rate them.
» Market Tour: Arrange a day to visit local farmers' markets with your group. Compare notes on the best deals and taste test.
» Parents: Go to a local farm and see how the crops go from the seeds in the field to dinner plates. Children will be engrossed with farming equipment, animals, and all of the work that goes into life on a farm.

POWER PROMOTION

» Place flyers for the program in books about shopping locally, organic lifestyles, and health foods.
» Ask other local businesses to post flyers as part of a community effort to "Buy Local."
» Make sure to publicize that samples of fresh produce will be tasted at this community event.

LGBT PRIDE MONTH

Every June, Lesbian, Gay, Bisexual, and Transgender (LGBT) Pride Month is celebrated to commemorate the 1969 Stonewall riots that began the Gay Liberation movement in the United States (see www.loc.gov/lgbt/about.html for more information). Create a learning opportunity for teens and adults with this program about various LGBT organizations and advocacy options. Key themes identified in this book are education and information, and this is a great chance to show support for this often underserved population.

PREPARATION TIME	LENGTH OF PROGRAM	NUMBER OF PATRONS	SUGGESTED AGE RANGE
1–2 hours	1 hour: 45 minutes for panel discussion, 15 minutes for questions and answers	20–50	Older Teens–40s and Beyond

SHOPPING LIST

» Coffee

» Water

» Paper cups

SETUP

2 Months Before
» Contact LGBT organizations and ask representatives to speak at a panel discussion about ways to support the LGBT community.
» Seek out various organizations and nonprofits that operate on the local, state, and national levels.

1 Week Before
» Create a handout of helpful resources and places to find information for people who identify as LGBT or allies. Include hotlines, online resources, testimonials, health information, statistics, education, and information about supporting LGBT friends or family members.
» Ask presenters if they require any technology equipment or special setup.
» Come up with questions for the panel in case there is a break in the discussion. Here are some sample questions:
  – What are different ways, both in person and online, to support the LGBT community and be an active ally?
  – What are the newest laws for the state? For the country?
  – What are some challenges that LGBT youth face that straight teens don't?

– What are some issues with bullying, both online and in person?
– What companies are champions for LGBT rights?
– What do you think is the future for LGBT rights? What changes do you envision in five, ten, and twenty years?

1 Hour Before
» Set up a table and chairs at the front of the room.
» If needed, connect a microphone, speakers, and a laptop and presentation system.
» Make coffee to offer to presenters and guests.
» Pull LGBT fiction and nonfiction books from the collection and have them available for checkout.

MAKE IT HAPPEN

» Welcome and thank all speakers and supporters. Remind everyone that this is a safe space to speak and share ideas.
» Act as a moderator for the panel and ask the speakers how their organizations support the LGBT community, who their target audience is, how they are funded, what projects they are involved in, and how people can help.
» Allow the discussion to flow among participants, but be prepared with a list of questions in case there is a lull in the conversation.
» Ask the speakers how the library can become an ally and what librarians can do to facilitate discussion and advocacy in the community.
» Take questions from the audience. Allow time for people to ask the speakers questions privately after the panel has disbanded.
» Encourage patrons to peruse and check out LGBT-themed books.

VARIATIONS

» Pride Parade: Coordinate with other librarians or libraries to participate in the local Pride parade. Show that libraries are a proud ally of the LGBT movement.
» Online: Change the library logo or mascot on social media to include a positive message or rainbow flags supporting LGBT rights and Pride Month.
» Older Teens: Create a teen panel with allies and organization members who work directly with young adults. Discover how teens can become actively involved in these organizations and become LGBT advocates and allies.

POWER PROMOTION

» Create a display of LGBT books and create bookmark flyers advertising the program.
» Market this program to junior high and high school teachers. Send information to the local schools and encourage administrators and teachers to attend.

REALISTIC SUMMER READING AND MEDIA PROGRAMS FOR ADULTS

MANY ADULTS ARE shy about participating in summer reading programs, thinking staff will judge their reading selection or how slowly they read. Parents bring their kids in to sign up and participate in summer reading but do not sign up themselves, thinking they are too busy with the kids' activities. This section offers some suggestions to encourage different age groups of adults with user-friendly options.

All of the ages covered in this book could benefit from some aspects of summer reading:

» Allow different types of media, from audiobooks to movies to CDs. Some libraries have listening or viewing programs just for special media with prizes tailored to those interests—for example, raffles for iTunes or an MP3 player. Programs that allow all types of media in addition to books are the most flexible and likely the most appealing to busy adults.

» Give credit for attending library programs. In a popular program at the Schaumburg Township District Library, adults can record attendance at any library event, from ones they may bring their children to through concerts or adult cooking demonstrations or computer classes.

» Online participation is necessary to attract younger adults, and it should be consistently working and easily accessible from the library home page. Paper logs may still be desired by some patrons, and it is easy enough to make simple logs or bookmarks with spaces to record books, media, or programs. The Events software (http://evancedsolutions.com) has forms and registration options for online reading programs, and other software may as well. Patrons should not be required to write reviews. If the library is concerned that people are cheating, keep in mind that the majority of people are not.

» Registration should be easy and fast. If people register online, send them a message to pick up their prize the next time they come in. Staff can just check them off on computerized or online forms in Events or another software program after they pick it up. A table in the lobby where all ages can register for the first week or two of the event is a good way to get attention.

» Sign-up prizes really get adults to commit. Make the sign-up prizes easy to carry in a pocket or purse, or extremely useful. This is easier said than done of course, but popular prizes at the Schaumburg Township District Library have included containers of mints or lip balms, cell phone cases with clips, pens, and pads of

paper. Other libraries have donated T-shirts available for all ages who register for their program.

» Promotions: Although adults may not be able to check in every week or two as many children's programs require, a midpoint drawing or incentive keeps momentum going in the program. Consider also e-mail notices or Facebook group updates about the program, including upcoming events or new media.

TARGET GROUPS

In this section, we discuss summer reading programs that may appeal especially to particular groups of patrons.

Older Teens

Engaging teens in summer reading is often a challenging yet rewarding process. As stated earlier, this is often difficult because of the many changes and pressures teens face today (summer school, sports, family and friend obligations, jobs, and more). Make summer reading as simple and as streamlined as possible to benefit both teens and staff.

Keep in touch with school staff and have a presence at local schools. Have sign-ups during lunch hours at the high schools and offer incentives, such as free ice cream treats or candy bars. Many high school students are required to read at least one book during summer break, and many use the library to find books. Use this opportunity to promote summer reading—they will already have read one book. If you have a summer reading collection, place flyers and sign-up sheets in books or on the shelf.

Extend summer reading to include more than reading—include attending library programs and teen events. Libraries are more than book repositories; they hold experiences waiting to happen. Many of the programs in the Community College Connections Club (see the Clubs That Keep Them Coming Back chapter) can be adapted to suit older teens' needs. Allow some of these programs and clubs to be used in lieu of reading a book. Teens will still be using the library and its resources and forming a personal connection with the library. This option also helps with the limited free time teens have. A book may take weeks to read, and teens may find it a challenge to read more than one or two each summer, but it takes less time and investment to attend a few teen programs over the course of the summer.

Give teens options. There is no right fit for every teen, and what may interest a 13-year-old girl may not generate the same enthusiasm from an 18-year-old high school senior. Allow teens to choose from a variety of prizes. Have your Teen Advisory Board offer input and vote on prizes. Offer prizes at different levels so as not to discourage those who feel it is too difficult to finish: have prizes for sign-up, midway, and completion.

20s and 30s

Garnering participation in your summer reading program from the 20s and 30s crowd in a manner that is effective for you and beneficial and relevant to them involves a combination of the ideas throughout this book. Off-site programming and a targeted reading group related to your program theme are potential directions in which you can go, as is tying in your regularly scheduled programming (perhaps a trivia night or a book discussion group that is already under way).

Depending on your summer reading theme, you could choose a book (or multiple books) within that theme that also has particular appeal for the 20s and 30s crowd and hold a series of discussions—a sort of book club in miniseries form. Although it's difficult to generalize what constitutes "particular appeal" for this demographic, consider books by authors who don't have huge commercial appeal and who write about topics that might not be covered in more traditional library book clubs. In other words, think about "safe" book discussion books and go in the opposite direction. Furthermore, consider holding the discussions off-site at a local bar or coffee shop.

Consider creating additional programming unique to the 20s and 30s crowd that ties into the summer reading theme. Holding these programs out of the library is a great way to encourage participation among patrons who aren't necessarily interested in coming into the library and signing up for the program. You can have registration and information available at the programs for the convenience of attendees.

Power Parenting Program: Surviving Summer Reading

Parents are always looking for strategies to survive the summer! Offering a program that rewards them or rewards families may be an activity they all enjoy. A family summer event may reward stories listened to or read together, movies watched, programs attended, and more. One member of the family can register, putting information about the ages of other members in the notes column. Prizes can include vouchers for clearing the overdue fines for all members or bonus coupons for checking out extra DVDs or video games if those items have limits. Local food coupons are always popular and can often be solicited, but they should not require most of the family to pay for a meal or incur other costs.

The family reading program can be done in addition to the individual programs and can have weekly trivia or quick games for bonus raffles. For example, if the family downloads an audiobook from the website and sends in the name, they get a raffle entry. Or if they sign up for the library Twitter feed and mention a book one or all of them enjoyed. Or if they ask for the website link to homework or job searching help on the library website. Invite program members to renew an item in their account and send the name of it for another entry. These interactive activities teach patrons about useful services from the library while allowing easy participation with incentives.

Something for Everyone

Summer is a great time to remind adults how the library can make their lives easier—and more fun.

JULY

HOT TOPICS WILL bring patrons in out of the heat this summer.

Many younger adults are learning how to outfit their first homes or how to cook for themselves or their families. DIY Decorating on a Dime will help those who have recently moved into new apartments or homes or simply want to update their current home. The Quick and Easy Recipe Swap or the Microwave Magic and Easy-Bake Oven Adventures class will bring out seasoned and wanna-be chefs.

Other adults heading into vacations are looking for something to read. Literary Speed Dating matches books and people in a unique way.

Help adults save money and time while they enjoy themselves at unique programs this month.

DIY DECORATING ON A DIME

Decorating one's living space can be challenging in general, but it can be even trickier when working with a limited budget. Repurposing items from flea markets and thrift stores certainly isn't a new concept, but it can be intimidating to someone who is just getting started. This program combines both of these potential obstacles with tips and tricks for making the most of a space as well as pulling off effective secondhand shopping.

PREPARATION TIME	LENGTH OF PROGRAM	NUMBER OF PATRONS	SUGGESTED AGE RANGE
2 hours	1½ hours	25	20s–30s

SHOPPING LIST

- » Water
- » Tea
- » Coffee
- » Cookies
- » Crackers
- » Cheese
- » Paper plates
- » Napkins

SETUP

2–3 Months Before

- » Find a presenter or multiple presenters who can cover the topics of DIY home decorating as well as making the most of one's living space. As with many other programs suggested in this book, you may be able to find a presenter among your colleagues at the library.
- » If no one among the staff feels comfortable leading the program, perhaps a former library presenter would be fit for the job. You can check out local craft stores to see what presenters they have on staff.

1 Hour Before

- » Set up the refreshments table.
- » Also set up a table of books similar to those on your promo display (see the Power Promotion section at the end of this program) to provide further inspiration. Be sure to let your patrons know that the books are available for checkout!

MAKE IT HAPPEN

» This is essentially a straightforward, presenter-led program. It will be up to your presenter(s) to decide how to tackle these topics in a cohesive manner, but you can provide suggestions and guidance to make sure that it is the program you envisioned it to be.

VARIATIONS

» Rather than having a presenter lead the program, consider making it more of a DIY/design hack share-a-thon, in which participants bring their own tips and tricks to share with the group. They can even bring examples of their work to show.

» Consider holding this program in conjunction with a Crafterwork program (see the Clubs That Keep Them Coming Back chapter) and provide materials so that participants can try out some of the suggested DIY projects.

POWER PROMOTION

» Create a book display of DIY crafting books and interior design books. Include on the display information about the program.

» Reach out to local craft and thrift stores and ask to advertise the program in those establishments.

QUICK AND EASY RECIPE SWAP

A recipe swap is an easy way to spice up one's culinary repertoire, and just about everyone is on the lookout for especially quick and simple recipes for weekday meals.

PREPARATION TIME	LENGTH OF PROGRAM	NUMBER OF PATRONS	SUGGESTED AGE RANGE
1 hour	1½ hours	25	20s–30s

SHOPPING LIST

» Recipe cards » Pens

SETUP

2 Months Before
» When you begin to advertise for the program, make sure to mention that participants should bring enough copies of each recipe to equal the maximum registration number so that everyone will be sure to receive a recipe.
» Also be sure to state what kinds of recipes are the focus of the program (for example, quick and easy entrees or desserts).

1 Week Before
» Shop for supplies.

1 Hour Before
» Set up your program space so that the chairs are arranged in a circle.
» Place the recipe cards and pens on a table in case they are necessary (they may or may not be).

MAKE IT HAPPEN

» Have everyone sit in the circle of chairs. Invite participants to stand up one at a time and describe their recipe—including any tips or tricks for making it a success—as the copies are passed around to the group.

» Some participants might have brought more than one recipe, but if you have a large group and time is a concern, you might want to start by having each person do only one recipe at a time until everyone has presented once.

VARIATIONS

» It is not necessary for your participants to bring in a ready-made dish from their recipe to provide samples, but it also doesn't hurt!

» Consider adding another element to the program by hiring a local chef to discuss cooking for one or two people in particular and to possibly provide a cooking demonstration.

POWER PROMOTION

» Create a book display of cookbooks, especially those that feature quick and easy recipes and cooking small meals for one or two people, and include information about the program.

MICROWAVE MAGIC AND EASY-BAKE OVEN ADVENTURES

Part of this program is reprinted with permission from *A Year of Programs for Teens 2* by Amy Alessio and Kimberly Patton. New recipes appealing to adults in their 20s and 30s have been added.

PREPARATION TIME	LENGTH OF PROGRAM	NUMBER OF PATRONS	SUGGESTED AGE RANGE
3 hours shopping and setup	2 hours	20–25	20s–30s

SHOPPING LIST

» At least two microwave ovens and an Easy-Bake oven with at least 2 little cake pans are necessary for this program.
» Measuring spoons

» Microwavable plates, bowls
» Cups or bottled water
» Plastic or permanent silverware

Baked Apples

» 2–3 types of apples, sliced with peels
» Shredded cheddar
» Raisins
» Cinnamon
» Nutmeg
» Margarine sticks

» Brown sugar
» White sugar
» Optional: caramel candies or caramel apple wrap, chocolate chips, butterscotch chips, seasonal sprinkles

Nachos

» 2–3 types of corn chips
» 2–3 types of cheese, including Velveeta
» Hormel canned chili
» Refried beans

» Green and black olives
» 2–3 types of salsa
» Chili powder
» Green chili peppers
» Hot sauce

Haystacks

- » Chocolate chips
- » Butterscotch chips
- » Peanut butter
- » Pretzel sticks
- » Chow mein noodles
- » Mini marshmallows
- » M&Ms
- » Raisins

Popcorn Pizzazz (Cheesy Popcorn, Caramel Balls)

- » Microwavable popcorn bags
- » Mini marshmallows
- » 3 sticks butter
- » Caramel ice cream sauce
- » Shredded cheddar (can also be used for quesadillas)
- » Grated Parmesan

Easy-Bake Oven Quesadillas

- » (Toppings from microwaved nachos can also be used here.)
- » Tortillas
- » Shredded cheddar cheese

Mini Cakes

- » 4 cake mixes
- » Milk
- » 3 tubs frosting
- » Decorator icing tubes (optional) or candies to decorate

SETUP

2 Months Before

- » Plan the menu and types of snacks for the event.
- » Begin publicity, targeting grocery stores, cooking classes at the park district, and cafés in particular.

1 Week Before

- » Shop for food and paper goods.
- » Test recipes and take digital photos. Although it may seem like a better idea to do this well in advance and then have photos for printed publicity, shopping closer to the date ensures the appropriate grocery products will be available. For example, fall sprinkles for the haystacks or apples will not be available all the time, nor will particular types of apples.

1 Hour Before

- » Set up each station for four to five adults by putting all the ingredients for one recipe on each table. Prep foods as necessary (for example, slice the apples).
- » Put out water on each table for palate cleansing.

MAKE IT HAPPEN

» As adults come in, direct them to a prep station for either the microwave ovens or the Easy-Bake oven.
» Make copies of each group's favorite recipes and hand them out at the end.

Baked Apples

» Participants should begin by putting several apple slices in a microwavable bowl. Then they can put some brown or white sugar, raisins, cinnamon, nutmeg, or melted margarine over the apples. If they choose to add cheese, they can do that after the initial "baking" of the apples.
» Each group should microwave their apples for about 3–3½ minutes until tender. (Different types of apples may have different cooking times.) If participants choose to add cheese, they can do so now and zap the bowl again for another 15 seconds.
» Back at their table, participants can rate the flavor combination they chose. Encourage participants to make this dish one more time with a different combination. For example, an apple dessert can be made by melting caramel candies, caramel apple wraps, or chocolate or butterscotch chips in the microwave, drizzling them over the apples, and then adding seasonal sprinkles such as fall leaves.

Nachos

» Participants can try different combinations of chips, salsa toppings, cheese, black and green olives, refried beans, Hormel canned chili, Velveeta cheese, chili peppers, or chili powder. The dish should be microwaved for no more than 1 minute, or just until the cheese bubbles.
» Again, participants can vote on the flavor combination and try again.

Haystacks

» Participants will first need to melt chocolate chips, butterscotch chips, or other types of chips with ¼ cup peanut butter for 45 seconds, until the mixture can be easily stirred. Then they can add pretzels, chow mein noodles, mini marshmallows, M&Ms, raisins, and more.

Popcorn Pizzazz

» Eight to ten participants can work at this station, with one group making the cheesy popcorn and the other the caramel balls.
  – Cheesy Popcorn: This group will first pop the popcorn and then toss it immediately with ¾ cup shredded cheddar and at least 3 tablespoons of Parmesan.
  – Caramel Balls: This group will first melt 4 tablespoons of butter. Then they will pop the popcorn in the microwave. The popcorn should be tossed with the butter immediately after popping. Then they will lightly microwave the mini marshmallows for 20 seconds at a time, watching to make sure the

marshmallows do not get too large and messy. The marshmallows will be combined with the popcorn and formed into balls. The caramel sauce can be drizzled on top.

Easy-Bake Oven Quesadillas

» This group will put shredded cheese between two layers of tortillas and "bake" for 20 seconds, or until cheese melts.

Mini Cakes

» Chefs will combine 3 tablespoons of cake mix with 1 tablespoon of milk and pour the mixture into a greased pan (to grease pans, use the wrappers from the sticks of butter or spray with Pam).
» Two cake pans should fit in most Easy-Bake ovens at a time and should bake for 15 minutes.
» Adults can work in teams to bake and decorate cakes as desired before sharing.

VARIATIONS

» Iron Chef Microwave Style: Invite each table to have their creations "judged" by a predetermined panel on presentation and taste.
» Healthy Snacks: Swap sugary, high-fat snacks and recipes for healthier choices, especially for the microwave, including trail mix Healthy Haystacks, popcorn balls with honey or peanut butter, and so on.
» Microwave Magic or Easy-Bake Oven Adventures with Demonstrations Only: Demonstrate each recipe using a projector, slides, or a mirror so all can see and hand out pre-made samples (be sure there are enough samples for everyone).

POWER PROMOTION

» Hand out a recipe for the Baked Apples with the program information on the back at programs for 20s and 30s before this event.
» Put up posters in grocery stores, cafés, and the like.
» Consider wearing an apron at work (or hanging one up at the reference and checkout desks) for several days before the event to boost questions or registration. Adults may not ask outright, but they will notice.

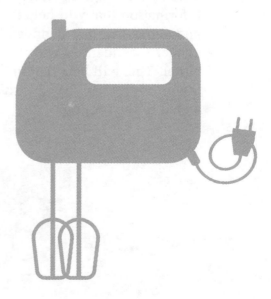

LITERARY SPEED DATING

Romance goes beyond the stacks with a speed dating program at the library. Many people want opportunities to meet others outside of noisy bars or clubs, and the library provides the perfect setting to bring like-minded individuals together. Connect fans of the written word at this event for lonely hearts, no matter what their taste is in books. Invite people to bring their favorite book—even if a match is not true love, they can at least chat about their books.

PREPARATION TIME	LENGTH OF PROGRAM	NUMBER OF PATRONS	SUGGESTED AGE RANGE
2–3 hours	1½ hours	40–50	20s–30s

SHOPPING LIST

» Name tags
» Permanent markers
» Pens
» Chocolate kisses
» Twinkle lights
» Flowers
» Vases
» CD player
» CD with silly love songs

SETUP

2 Months Before

» Begin promotion for the event: send out flyers to bars, coffee shops, train stations, and gyms.
» When people sign up, have them fill out a confidential online form requesting information that will help the program run smoothly: name; e-mail address and phone number (confidential and only given out if a match is made); age; gender they identify with; and whether they are looking for a male, female, or either. This will help determine if there are more females than males registering or if a lesbian, gay, bisexual, and transgender (LGBT) element should be added to the program.

1 Week Before

» Create scorecards for participants to match with one another:

Name: **JANE A.**		
	MATCH US!	**JUST FRIENDS**
JAMES K.	✖	
MATTHEW S.		✖
ALEX W.	✖	
RYAN B.		✖

» Make a handout of tips for conversation starters (for example, What are your favorite outdoor activities? What do you enjoy about your job? Do you like to travel?).

2 Hours Before

» Purchase flowers for tables and candy for people to snack on.
» Arrange tables into a large circle with chairs on the inside and outside that match the number of participants. Additional tables will be needed if you have LGBT participants.
» Place the flowers and chocolate kisses on the tables.
» Turn on the music and wait for people to arrive.

MAKE IT HAPPEN

» Welcome guests and ask them to put on a (pre-made) name tag with their first name and first letter of their last name. Each person gets a scorecard and pen. Make sure participants write their names on the scorecards.
» Ask the women to sit on the inside of the circle and the men to sit on the outside.
» Explain how Speed Dating will work. Each match will have a set time (usually 4–6 minutes) depending on how many participants you have. Participants should write the name of each "date" on the scorecard and, at the end of the designated time, if they like a person they should check the "Match Us!" box; otherwise, they should check the "Just Friends" box.
» At the end of each round, the men will stand up and move one seat to the right.
» Once everyone has made it around the table, ask participants to return the scorecards to staff members so that they can play matchmaker.
» After everyone has left, check the scorecards for matches. Send contact information to both parties if they both checked the "Match Us!" box.

VARIATIONS

» Host a singles mixer or an after-hours masquerade at the library. Encourage literary costumes or masks for a masquerade. This can also be done at an off-site location with a community partner.

» If you have a large LGBT population or high interest, consider hosting a separate LGBT Speed Dating program. The program would largely be the same, but additional tables would be needed specific to gender identity and attraction, and patrons who are attracted to the same sex would need to rotate to meet all individuals of that gender.

POWER PROMOTION

» Place an ad on social media or dating websites—this often reaches a larger audience in your neighborhood, including people who normally don't frequent the library, and can even target people who are single.

» Post flyers in bars, coffee shops, train stations, and gyms to draw in a male crowd.

8

AUGUST

BACK-TO-SCHOOL TIME MEANS parents' schedules change. New classes and schools start soon, and two library programs can help with these issues. Ways to Work from Home presents options for parents returning to the workplace or seeking to earn extra money while the kids are at school. Life in Elementary, Middle, and High School offers parents a chance to meet local school administrators and students and to have pressing questions answered.

Not everyone is headed back to school. People in their 20s and 30s may have just finished degrees and are ready to brave the Karaoke Night and Shark Week Celebration interactive events.

Continue to educate, entertain, and inspire with a variety of August ideas.

POWER PARENTING
WAYS TO WORK FROM HOME

Finding a job that is flexible around school schedules is challenging. Parents may find that working from home is an option. This program will present some legitimate situations that may allow for paid work from home. Résumé writing and query letters will also be reviewed.

PREPARATION TIME	LENGTH OF PROGRAM	NUMBER OF PATRONS	SUGGESTED AGE RANGE
1 hour preparing material	1 hour	30	30s–40s

SHOPPING LIST

No supplies are needed, but a computer and projector will be necessary on the day of the program.

SETUP

1 Month Before
» Put the presentation together, double-checking sites and resources.
» Brochure copy describing the program should invite participants to bring in a sample résumé and query letter for feedback.

1 Week Before
» Pull library materials on freelance writing markets, making money from crafts, eBay selling, investing basics, résumé writing, and job searching.

1 Hour Before
» Set up the computer and projector.

» As people come in, take names of those who would like feedback on their résumés and query letters. If only a few wish to participate in that activity, there will be time to cover all of them. If many do, indicate that people will exchange in small groups and help each other.

» Open the presentation by asking who has earned money working from home, what they did, and how they found that type of work. Suggest that former employment may have opportunities. Many companies desire employees for whom they may not have to pay benefits or provide office space. Discuss the feasibility of proposing some part-time work from home to former employers.

Ways to Work from Home Topics

Growing an Online Platform

» It is possible to make money from ads while blogging or from YouTube videos. This process may require setup costs and can take time. Many people who are successful bloggers and marketers offer free webinars. The following are some good resources from people who have built very successful freelance online businesses:
  – http://problogger.com
  – http://patflynn.com
  – http://beafreelanceblogger.com
  – www.firepolemarketing.com

eBay

» Selling things on eBay can be hit or miss, but plenty of people make cash from things in their homes. Suggest that participants look at what they have, especially in collections like old toys, and see if it is selling on eBay. Even more modern things like old Coach purses or Thomas the Tank Engine trains have a lot of interest. Participants can begin making cash quickly on eBay, and the site has an easy-to-use setup form.

» This resource has a lot of information and is comprehensive: www.skipmcgrath .com/auction_sr/77-tips-tools-selling-ebay.shtml.

Etsy

» This site continues to grow. Again, have participants look at what is selling and how people market. If attendees have exceptional or unique skills, this may be a good option.

Telecommuting Opportunities

» FlexJobs (www.flexjobs.com) is a subscription service that lists telecommuting jobs, including tutoring, medical coding, and more. Viewers can look at opportunities without subscribing but must pay to apply.

Offering Webinars or Online Classes

» Many organizations are looking for people to offer online webinars or training. The American Library Association, Romance Writers of America, and medical organizations take proposals for classes, then keep a percentage. They handle the technical aspects on their end (teachers must have a good headset and computer). Some people get their own meeting space software and offer classes from their blog or off their YouTube videos. Participants should attend one or two 1-hour webinars to get a feel for how they are run. Most run off PowerPoint with voice discussion. Some allow for questions and answers on chat or other methods. Attendees can pay via PayPal, and the teacher does all the advertising. This is a great option if a person has built up a name freelancing for a while. Starting with an organization is a good way to learn to do webinars.

» Online classes involve e-mail or online bulletin boards where the teacher puts up lessons and discussion questions for students to address. The teacher has to log on daily and may also assign projects.

Tutoring or Teaching Students Face-to-Face

» Suggest that people who may be considering this option double-check their household insurance policies. Music lessons or tutoring could be done in the home.

Résumés and Query Letters

» Ask attendees to form small groups to critique (nicely) each other's résumés and query letters.

VARIATIONS

» Write a short article with links for library social media on this topic and invite people to share places that have hired them to work from home successfully.

» Series: If attendees are particularly interested in how to teach webinars or online classes, that could be a separate session. Freelance markets and writing would be another one. If interest demands, more time can be devoted to favorite topics.

POWER PROMOTION

» Place information on this program on any back-to-school or fall media displays in the library.

» Post flyers and information regarding the program on social media, particularly the Youth Services section.

POWER PARENTING
LIFE IN ELEMENTARY, MIDDLE, AND HIGH SCHOOL

Although many schools have parent and child visits or orientation in the spring, many questions still may be unanswered. At this event, 30 minutes each is spent on elementary, middle, and high school life at the local public schools. Administrators or staff members, or both, will be speaking, and students and parents as well. This should be advertised as a program about daily life in school and not necessarily about academics.

PREPARATION TIME	LENGTH OF PROGRAM	NUMBER OF PATRONS	SUGGESTED AGE RANGE
2 hours	1¾ hours: 30 minutes for each school with 5-minute breaks in between	75 (or what the meeting area will comfortably hold)	Parents with children

SHOPPING LIST

» Index cards and pencils for questions (optional)
» Thank-you gifts for panelists and speakers (such as candy, fine-free coupons, books)

SETUP

3–6 Months Before
» Contact one or two elementary, middle, and high schools in the library area and ask if an administrator would be available to give a brief 5- to 10-minute presentation about things families and students need to know about that level of school.
» Poll staff members or library regulars to see if they and their children could participate on a panel about any of the schools. Teen volunteers are another good source. If a few people are not found for each of the schools, ask the school parent organization for more volunteers. They should be prepared to discuss parking, extracurricular activities, options for free periods throughout the day, buses, lunchtime, lockers, ways for parents to get involved, and more.

1 Week Before

» Double-check with all speakers to ensure they know what time they are speaking.

1 Hour Before

» Check audiovisual equipment, especially the computer and projector if needed, and microphones for the panelists.

MAKE IT HAPPEN

» For each segment, invite audience members to write questions on cards to be passed to the panelists. Collect those throughout the program and let the panelists choose among them if there are several.
» Introduce administrators or school representatives for their brief presentation first, then panel members. You may choose to moderate panels and field questions informally from the audience.
» At the end of each 30-minute section, show audience members relevant homework help sections of the library website or in the library before setting up for the next group.

VARIATIONS

» Private Schools: Representatives from private schools can hold a session. This can also be held in February when registration is occurring.
» Homeschooling: Local homeschool families can discuss different age levels of curriculum, standards, and tips.

POWER PROMOTION

» Place bookmarks with information on this event on all reserve items a week before the event—for all ages.
» Place signs and flyers in the adult, youth, and teen areas.
» Ask local schools to help by advertising at their orientation days in early August if possible.

KARAOKE NIGHT

Show off your patrons' singing skills (or lack thereof) in a laughter-filled night of music and snacks at the library. Hosting an after-hours or late-night karaoke fest is a good way to bring energy and life into the library. Capitalize on the popularity of musicals, Disney, a cappella singing, Broadway, and more with a Karaoke Night.

PREPARATION TIME	LENGTH OF PROGRAM	NUMBER OF PATRONS	SUGGESTED AGE RANGE
1½ hours	2–3 hours	20–30	Older Teens

SHOPPING LIST

- » Snacks
- » Soda
- » Bottled water
- » Paper plates
- » Napkins
- » Speakers

- » Pencils
- » Scorecards
- » Karaoke machine or computer and speaker with CD drive
- » Microphones (1–2)

SETUP

2 Months Before
- » Determine if you want to use a karaoke machine or a computer that can play karaoke music and display the lyrics on-screen.
- » If using a computer, you may have to download additional software. One advantage of using a computer, or a tablet and karaoke app, is instantaneous access to thousands of songs. Another option is to rent a karaoke machine.

1 Week Before
- » Gather and test the equipment and check out multiple karaoke CDs from different genres. Buy all nonperishable snacks and goods. Allow sign-ups online or at the reference desk if you anticipate a large crowd.
- » Create sign-up cards that include name, song title, and the artist and print out multiple copies to distribute for the event. Create karaoke scorecards: "Most original interpretation," "Best dancer," "Best duet," "Funniest performance," and so on.

1 Hour Before

» Move furniture into an inviting atmosphere—create a stage and audience seating.
» Place pencils, karaoke request slips, and scorecards at tables.
» Set up the karaoke equipment and microphones near the stage.

MAKE IT HAPPEN

» Have music playing when people walk in. Hand out song request slips to people as they walk in and encourage them to grab snacks.
» Let the karaoke night begin and call up the first few participants.
» Make sure the songs chosen are available with the CDs or computer and app. If not, present performers with their options and ask them to choose from the selection.
» After each performance, acknowledge the person, clap, and thank the individual. Remind audience members to vote for their favorite performances.
» Take a break from karaoke and play a game of "Name That Song." Play the first few seconds of a song and have people guess the song title and artist. Participants can form teams or do this individually.
» With a braver crowd, play karaoke roulette and have audience members pick songs for the performers before they come to the microphone.

VARIATIONS

» Have a themed karaoke night and only play songs from a specific decade or genre. Encourage people to wear costumes.
» Seek out a local piano bar and ask whether a piano player would provide an entertaining evening of live music for a sing-along. Use a piano or keyboard for music.
» Host a musical sing-along with classic or popular, quotable movies.

POWER PROMOTION

» Place flyers near the karaoke CDs, sheet music, or music DVDs in the library's AV collection.
» Promote this event at Teen Advisory Board meetings and send flyers to the local high schools.
» Put flyers in teen books that highlight music, such as *Just Listen* by Sarah Dessen, *If I Stay* by Gayle Forman, *Five Flavors of Dumb* by Antony John, *Eleanor and Park* by Rainbow Rowell, and *This Song Will Save Your Life* by Leila Sales.

SHARK WEEK CELEBRATION

Discovery Channel's Shark Week seems to grow in popularity each year. It also provides a great opportunity for a pop culture–heavy social and entertainment program.

LENGTH OF PROGRAM	NUMBER OF PATRONS	SUGGESTED AGE RANGE
2+ hours	30	20s–30s

PREPARATION TIME

2 hours shopping and setup (plus additional time to find and hire a presenter, if applicable)

SHOPPING LIST

» Snacks (Gummy blue sharks, Goldfish crackers, Lifesavers candy, tortilla chips, salsa, fresh fruit mix including strawberries and blueberries)
» Paper plates
» Napkins
» Beverages (water, tea, coffee, soda)

SETUP

2 Months Before
» Decide on what elements you are going to incorporate into your program.
» If you plan to feature a presentation from a professional, start reaching out to people in the area to see who is interested and available.

1 Week Before
» Shop for supplies.

1 Hour Before
» Set up snack table and cue up the movie you're planning to show.

MAKE IT HAPPEN

Shark Trivia

» Start off with an abbreviated trivia session about all things shark related (see Trivia Nights in the Clubs That Keep Them Coming Back chapter for inspiration). Mix it up by asking earnest shark questions as well as questions about the myriad sharks present in popular culture. Make sure you have some shark-tastic prizes to hand out to winners.

Movie Screening

» Sit back and enjoy the show! It's hard to go wrong with a screening of the mother of all shark movies, *Jaws*, but there's also no shortage of terror-in-the-deep films that you could show instead.

VARIATIONS

» For an added element of education (possibly in lieu of viewing a shark film), reach out to colleges, zoos, or aquariums in your area to ask a professional to speak about sharks. (*Note*: Including this in your program might require you to adjust your program length.)
» If you aren't able to bring someone into the library, explore your options for setting up a Skype session with a professional.

POWER PROMOTION

Create a display of shark-related fiction and nonfiction books as well as DVDs and include on it information about the program.

9

SEPTEMBER

SEPTEMBER IS A time of change, from seasons to schedules, with many people going back to school or off to college. It is becoming more popular in this country for young adults to take a year in between high school and college to explore interests. Many of their peers and friends are heading off to start a new chapter of their lives, so now is a good time to reach out to those taking a gap year by showing them what is available through a Gap Year Fair.

People in their 20s and 30s are now mostly out of school and adjusting to life without a back-to-school rush. This can be a particularly challenging time for those diagnosed on the autism spectrum who may find their new social lives challenging. Consider offering a gaming night just for Adults Facing Social Challenges to help meet the needs of your community.

Summer may now be officially over, but that just means the start of fun fall activities! Bonfire Night may not seem like a library event, but wait until your patrons try this one. It is a great way to kick off the start of fall! People are always looking forward to vacation, and planning for the next family vacation is just beginning in September. Parents will enjoy a presentation of Tips for Traveling with Children.

Help patrons prepare for fall and the future this month with these programming ideas.

GAP YEAR FAIR

A gap year is a period, usually post–high school or college, when a student spends time volunteering, traveling, learning about other cultures, exploring areas of interest, and in general filling in the gaps of her or his education. This is a common practice for high school graduates in Europe and is becoming more popular and accepted in the United States. It is not about ending a student's education—it's about discovering who she is as a person and defining her place in the world, where she wants to go, and how she wants to get there. A Gap Year Fair gives options to students who are burnt out after graduation, are unsure of their career choices, want to travel, or make a difference in the world.

PREPARATION TIME	NUMBER OF PATRONS	SUGGESTED AGE RANGE
2 hours	20–50	Older Teens–20s

LENGTH OF PROGRAM

2 hours: 45 minutes to 1 hour for presentation (depending on number of speakers), 15 minutes for questions, 1 hour for Gap Year Fair.

SHOPPING LIST

» Name tags   » Pencils   » Name cards

SETUP

2 Months Before
» Contact organizations that specialize in youth volunteer programs and gap years. Some examples are AmeriCorps, the Peace Corps, and the American Gap Association.
» Ask representatives from gap year organizations, high school guidance counselors, and young adults who have taken gap years to speak about their experiences.

1 Week Before

» Create a handout featuring the common types of gap years (volunteer, travel, adventure, internship, conservation, etc.) and organizations.
» Create name cards for the participating organizations.

1 Hour Before

» Set up the presentation system.
» Arrange the other half of the room for the Fair, which will follow the presentation.

MAKE IT HAPPEN

» Welcome speakers and audience members.
» Introduce the various topics: advantages and disadvantages of a gap year, types of gap year programs available, costs, housing, and so forth.
» Invite questions from the audience.
» Conduct the Gap Year Fair. Have the organizations and counselors pass out information and talk personally with students and families.

VARIATIONS

» Study Abroad: Many young adults want a chance to explore the world, but want the support of a school or an organization. Offer a Study Abroad program in conjunction with your local college.
» What to Do When You're in the Wrong Career: Offer alternative options for people who want to change jobs and careers. Discuss popular careers and offer résumé assistance and the chance to talk with career counselors, employment agencies, and graduate schools.

POWER PROMOTION

» This program is going to need cross-promoting at high schools and colleges. Make sure high school counselors are informed so they can share this with students they feel might benefit from a gap year.
» If you have many teens or 20-somethings interested in a gap year, find out their interests. Chances are they are interested in volunteering or traveling abroad. Cross-promote with other programs such as Europe on the Cheap or the Service Club.
» Create a wanderlust book display with travel books and travelogues. Advertise this program and include a globe, a map, and fake passports for an eye-catching effect.

PROGRAM FOR ADULTS FACING SOCIAL CHALLENGES

In setting out to do programming for people in their 20s and 30s, it is assumed that one of the goals is to reach a group whose needs are not typically met by traditional library programming. It is possible through this programming—along with support from relevant community partners and professionals—to reach a specific subset of the 20s and 30s population: adults with high-functioning autism or Asperger's syndrome or those facing other social challenges. Although support for those facing these social challenges is available from pre-K through high school graduation, in many communities it is not as widely available to people once they have entered their 20s. It is quite possible that these adults—many of whom might already be familiar with using the public library—will be attracted to programming that is specific to adults their age, which is great! However, some might be reluctant to participate in these programs because they are nervous about being around a group that they feel might be unwelcoming to someone facing social challenges. Although we, of course, would expect that *all* patrons, no matter what challenges they face, would be welcome at any library program, we also recommend taking a look at the needs of your community. What resources are available to this population? What needs are not being met? Could young adults with social challenges benefit from 20s and 30s programming that is geared specifically to them and their peers?

The template provided here is for a low-key game night, similar to Old-School Gaming in the January chapter, without the emphasis on the "old-school" aspect. The intent is to create a relaxed social atmosphere with plenty to do but no pressure to do any one thing.

LENGTH OF PROGRAM	NUMBER OF PATRONS	SUGGESTED AGE RANGE
1½ hours	25	20s–30s

PREPARATION TIME

2–3 hours shopping and setup (additional time will be required to lay the groundwork: researching the needs of the demographic in the community, talking with professionals, and seeking out potential community partners)

SHOPPING LIST

- » Refreshments (such as water, soda, tea, coffee, chips, crackers, cookies)
- » Name tags
- » Pens

SETUP

3–4 Months Before

- » As noted, this program is likely to depend on support and contributions from local organizations that also assist adults with autism or Asperger's syndrome and others facing social challenges. We strongly recommend that before you move forward with creating a program for this specific demographic, you reach out to these organizations and even meet with them to determine what role your library can play in meeting the needs of these adults. Maybe that role is to create social opportunities like the game night outlined here, but perhaps a greater need is for employment or life skills workshops. Gauging the needs of your community in this manner will help greatly in providing a direction for creating partnerships with relevant organizations that can provide support and assistance in making these programs successful.
- » In addition to providing information about the needs of the demographic, resources in your community can assist in training library staff, as many or most of them might not be well versed in dealing with patrons who face certain social challenges. Community resources staff may also be able to provide assistance in running the program itself.

1 Month Before

- » In addition to advertising the program through your library's traditional means, promotion for this program might depend on what resources in the community are available.
- » If there are organizations that already serve patrons in this demographic, reach out to them and ask if they will spread the word about your program (create a concise flyer with the pertinent information that you can send to them, which they may in turn distribute).

1 Week Before

- » Decide what games to include in the program. If you are going to provide video gaming options, take stock of the consoles you have at your disposal, along with the options you have for televisions.
- » Come up with a plan for gathering all the electronic equipment that you'll need for the program, as well as for moving it all into the program space.

2 Hours Before

» Move equipment into your program space. Plug everything in and test it to make sure it all works.
» Gather whatever games (video and board) you have on hand and make sure you take note of their titles, barcodes (if applicable), and conditions so that you'll know what you should be collecting at the end of the program.

MAKE IT HAPPEN

» As participants arrive, have them fill out a name tag and put it on. This will be helpful as everyone interacts with one another. Once you're ready to get the program started, it might be helpful to have participants introduce themselves.
» If you are going to incorporate video gaming into your program, you'll need a substantial amount of electronics. Holding the program in a large room with plenty of electrical outlet access will be key. Depending on the setup of your library, you might also have to move several televisions into one room.

VARIATIONS

» As we've noted, gaming is certainly not the only option for a program created for adults facing social challenges. Other social and entertainment options include a movie or trivia night.
» In addition to social and entertainment opportunities, you can, with the help of your partners in the community, investigate providing relevant life skills workshops.

POWER PROMOTION

» As mentioned, a good deal of your promotion will come through the ties you have in the community.
» If it is necessary that the people attending your program not require the assistance of an aide (which is recommended in most cases), be sure to include that requirement in your promotional material so as not to create any confusion.
» Also make sure to include the appropriate contact information for the library staff who are organizing the program. If interested parties have questions or are looking for more details, you'll want to be sure that they are connected with staff who are prepared to answer questions and provide additional information.

BONFIRE NIGHT

Celebrate Halloween and the changing seasons with a bonfire in your local nature center or outside the library if possible. Sitting around a campfire, eating s'mores, and sharing stories brings people together in a fun atmosphere. Many people in their 20s and 30s want participatory experiences, and a night of high engagement over a roaring fire will attract many library users, both new and old. Make sure you have a backup plan or location in case of inclement weather.

PREPARATION TIME	LENGTH OF PROGRAM	NUMBER OF PATRONS	SUGGESTED AGE RANGE
1–2 hours	2–3 hours	20–45	20s–30s

SHOPPING LIST

- » Bottled water
- » Graham crackers
- » Chocolate bars
- » Marshmallows
- » Roasting sticks

- » Paper plates
- » Paper cups
- » Napkins or wet wipes
- » Apple cider
- » Glow sticks

- » Mason jars
- » Scissors
- » Flashlights
- » Wood
- » Newspaper

SETUP

2 Months Before
- » Contact your local wildlife or nature center and arrange a bonfire night on the grounds.
- » Another option is to ask your library director whether it would be feasible to host the bonfire on library property. If you do not have a fire pit or access to one, ask other staff members if one is available to borrow. Secure proper permissions, check local laws and ordinances, and, if needed, get a permit or license for the bonfire.
- » Reach out to the storytelling community and ask for volunteers or hire a performer to tell scary stories.

1 Week Before
- » Create a schedule and shopping list for the event. Buy all nonperishable goods and confirm the date and time with the storytellers, nature center staff, or library director.

1 Hour Before

» Light the bonfire and get the fire roaring.
» Make sure you have a bucket of water for emergencies.
» Arrange chairs or benches around the bonfire.
» Set up two tables—one for apple cider and s'mores supplies and the other for glow stick crafting.

MAKE IT HAPPEN

» Greet patrons and encourage them to warm up by the fire and start roasting marshmallows for s'mores. Pass out the glow sticks.
» While people get comfortable and more join in, have the storytellers tell scary stories.
» Take a creepy walk through the woods in the nature center. If you have extra staff or highly engaged patrons, ask them to jump out and scare everyone.
» Invite participants to open the glow sticks with scissors and pour the contents into the mason jars. Shaking the jars mixes the colors for a cool effect.

VARIATIONS

» Older Teens: Create an end-of-school celebration for teens. Allow them to burn old notes or pictures.
» Encourage Halloween costumes and have a candy creation station with taffy apples or candy sushi.
» Celebrate Guy Fawkes Night and create a program series based on the English Gunpowder Plot of November 5, 1605. Burn a Guy Fawkes doll, recite the poem "The Fifth of November," and watch the movie *V for Vendetta*.

POWER PROMOTION

» Choose a catchy name and graphics to go along with your program that correlate to pop culture nostalgia (for example, Halloweentown Bonfire or Are You Afraid of the Dark?).
» Post flyers in haunted houses and Halloween stores.

POWER PARENTING
FROM LOCAL TRIPS TO DISNEY AND BEYOND—TIPS FOR TRAVELING WITH CHILDREN

This program is intended to help families with children travel more comfortably, with tips on types of hotel rooms, ideas for car or plane travel, basic information on some popular destinations, and budget savers.

PREPARATION TIME	LENGTH OF PROGRAM	NUMBER OF PATRONS	SUGGESTED AGE RANGE
3 hours shopping and setup	1½ hours	25	20s–30s

SHOPPING LIST

- » Snacks (Goldfish crackers, pretzels, granola bars, etc.)
- » Napkins
- » Paper plates

SETUP

2 Months Before
- » See if any staff members who have traveled with families would be willing to speak or provide tips.
- » Speakers are often available to give tips on traveling to Disney theme parks and that may be a possibility for this program, for part or all of the presentation.

1 Week Before
- » Pull library media on local destinations and popular farther destinations, such as Disney theme parks, national parks, and more.
- » Research and bookmark sites for Disney, Universal, LEGO parks, U.S. government passports, and local destinations (within one day's travel).
- » If there are websites on area festivals or guides to family fun, bookmark those as well.
- » Research a few map and travel planning apps. Make a bookmark with a list of those sites as a handout for the program, along with some simple tips on how to download media from the library website.

» Shop for some car or travel-type snacks, such as Goldfish crackers, pretzels, and granola bars. If there is a fun local hotspot that makes fudge, jelly beans, or something else that is family friendly, consider providing samples of that as well. That location may donate or offer a discount because you will be discussing that destination.

» Pull word puzzles and coloring sheets, clipboards or hard surfaces on which to do puzzles, and colored pencils.

1 Hour Before
» Make sure AV equipment is working.
» Set out snacks, plates, and napkins.

MAKE IT HAPPEN

» If parents bring children, offer word puzzles or coloring sheets with colored pencils and clipboards for the children to work on during the presentation. These are also a demonstration of what to do during the car ride.

» Local hotspots: Are any local event guides or periodicals available for parents to pick up in the library? In the Chicago area, Oaklee's Family Guide has print and online versions. There are suburban publications and more. These all detail fairs, festivals, water parks, and museum ideas. Make sure audience members know about these, both in print and online, and especially point out any coupons.

» Disney 101: Budget, then double it. Show Disney World and Disneyland websites. Show ticket options, and explain what park hopping is (paying extra for flexibility to visit more than one park a day) and how to book mealtime reservations (highly recommended). This only scratches the surface, but there are lots of good books and websites on planning for Disney. Show apps for Disney and other theme parks and mention their features, including wait times and maps.

» Universal and LEGO theme parks: Show websites and mention new features such as the Harry Potter areas.

» Traveling beyond the United States: Show the U.S. Passports and International Travel website (http://travel.state.gov/content/passports/english/passports/apply.html) and mention the difference between passports and passport cards (for travel to Canada and Mexico). Discuss how to get the photo taken in your area (hours, if available, at the local post office).

» Travel and map apps: Travel budget apps are available for families to plan how much they will need for food, souvenirs, and more. Map apps within destinations and globally are necessary in case planned routes go awry because of construction or other issues.

» Snacks: Car trips may require a cooler for fruit and drinks in addition to a separate bag for snacks. For plane travel, kids may pack a few simple, sealed snacks in their travel bags. Discuss the ones served at the program.

» Plane travel: Review the rules about what can and can't be brought onboard. Discuss rolling backpacks for kids, size of carry-on, how to check a stroller, and what to expect if people have not traveled by air in a while.

» Hotel rooms: Discuss options—from "suites" with half walls (which keep no noise in, meaning kids do not usually sleep) to separate bedrooms for parents to basic hotel rooms. Advise parents to search for hotels with free breakfasts and refrigerators and to research pet options and pool features.

» Downloadables: Review the free downloadable options from the library site and discuss how audiobooks can be played in the car.

» Chargers: Discuss options for the car and laptop (parents should bring it for movies if nothing else). If possible, show the different types of chargers families may need for vacations—one per device, an emergency one for out and about, another for the car, and one to plug into a laptop.

» Reading in the dark: Early risers may like Kindles with lights, book lights, and other options. Mention again how downloadable books can be read this way.

» Movie players for the car: Discuss options that may be available at local big-box or media stories, including ones with separate controls for separate seats. Advise about headphones.

VARIATIONS

» Speakers: Disney experts often give talks at libraries. Ask staff at other libraries in your area whether anyone has had such a speaker for a reference. Travel agents or local AAA representatives may be other good speakers.

» Online: Ask families for tips they have used or websites they found helpful.

POWER PROMOTION

» Display travel materials in the youth area to appeal to young families new to traveling.

» Put information about the program on bookmark-size "tickets."

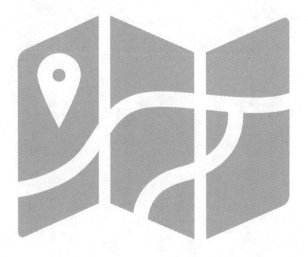

OCTOBER

AMID A BUSY fall filled with activities, adults may still be able to fit in programs on these timely topics.

The Clutter Doctor helps everyone pare down and get ready for the holidays, while the Virtual College Tours help parents and teens get ready for a more distant but crucial future.

Book fans can get together to share their love of butterbeer and other page-to-life creations amid the Fandom Frenzy, while those who just want to celebrate Halloween with other adults will enjoy looking back at a Throwback Halloween Night party.

Blending educational and recreational offerings keeps adults coming back for more.

CLUTTER DOCTOR

We all need a little help staying organized from time to time. This interactive program allows participants to get not only general advice for de-cluttering their homes and work spaces but also specific tips and solutions based on photos they have submitted of their own clutter problems.

PREPARATION TIME	LENGTH OF PROGRAM	NUMBER OF PATRONS	SUGGESTED AGE RANGE
3+ hours	1½ hours	20	20s–30s

SHOPPING LIST

» Pencils
» Paper

SETUP

2–3 Months Before

» Chances are you or others on your staff are great with organization. You can investigate hiring a personal organizer if you wish, but look at the resources available to you among your colleagues first. You might be surprised!

1 Month Before

» Advertise your program and let potential participants know that they can submit photos of their own clutter problems beforehand to get some specific suggestions based on what they are dealing with. Be sure to give them a "submit by" date to make sure that you will be able to put everything together in time for the program. It will be easiest if they submit digital photos, which you can then put into a PowerPoint presentation to show while they are receiving feedback. (Also be sure to let them know that the pictures will be used in such a presentation, though names will be removed.)

1 Week Before

» Compile the photos you have been sent into a PowerPoint in an order that makes sense (by room of the house, type of clutter, etc.).
» Send the PowerPoint presentation to the person who will be leading the program so that he or she can study the photos and prepare comments and suggestions ahead of time.

1 Hour Before

» Make sure the PowerPoint presentation is ready to go. Set out paper and pencils for participants to take notes, if they would like to.

MAKE IT HAPPEN

» Ask the presenter to give some basic organization tips to start—What day-to-day method(s) does she use to stay clutter-free? How does he tackle larger de-cluttering projects?
» Once the presenter has gone through some general information, turn to the PowerPoint of audience-submitted material. At this point, the presenter can go through the PowerPoint systematically and address issues presented in each picture (audience members do not have to claim ownership of any of the clutter, but can, of course, if they choose to).
» Once the presentation is complete, allow time for questions.

VARIATIONS

» It is an option, of course, to leave the user-submitted photos out of the equation and instead go for a straightforward organizational tips and tricks presentation.
» If your presenter has helpful storage supplies on hand, have her or him bring them for a bit of a show-and-tell, or consider adding pictures of helpful materials to the PowerPoint.

POWER PROMOTION

» Create a display of books and DVDs about organization and include on it information about the program.
» Consider including storage tubs and other organizational materials (and possibly a controlled bit of clutter) on the display to catch the eye of patrons.

POWER PARENTING
VIRTUAL COLLEGE TOURS

College tours can be intimidating for teens who don't yet know what they want to do or parents who are going through the process for the first time. Having local college representatives and slides from campus highlights in a library program can take some of the pressure off the process.

PREPARATION TIME	NUMBER OF PATRONS	SUGGESTED AGE RANGE
3 hours shopping and setup	50	Older Teens and parents

LENGTH OF PROGRAM

1½–2 hours, depending on how many schools participate. Plan on 15–20 minutes per presentation, with time for questions and an overview of online programs.

SHOPPING LIST

» Cookies for patrons, if desired

» Bottled water for all speakers

SETUP

3–6 Months Before
» Ask popular colleges within a few hours' driving distance of the library to participate with a presentation, visuals, handouts, and useful information about living options, scholarships, key programs, and extracurricular options such as ROTC in a 15- to 20-minute presentation each.
» Library staff could put together some basic information on local colleges if representatives are not available, especially if they send materials, but questions and answers would be more difficult.

1 Week Before
» Go over all details with speakers again.
» Pull information about online options and programs at the local colleges and beyond in popular fields.

1 Hour Before

» Ensure that all AV equipment is working and that each college has a place on a table to leave handouts for attendees.

MAKE IT HAPPEN

» As people arrive, show them where they can pick up handouts and invite them to sign up at the different school tables for e-mail lists if the colleges have this option.
» Keep each school on time with 15- to 20-minute presentations and a few questions each.

VARIATIONS

» Online: A school a week could be featured with an e-mail address and links for a participating staff member at the school who will answer particular questions for library patrons.
» Nighttime and Online: Ask colleges to present this same program format with an emphasis on older adult learners who are going back to school while keeping up with careers and families.

POWER PROMOTION

» Play college songs in the AV areas the week before the event and place handouts nearby.
» Place signs in the teen area and by the checkout desk or drive-thru, or both, to catch attention.
» Ask schools to help promote the event at their guidance offices.
» Many school districts have online "virtual backpack" options for outside groups, but they may still allow announcements to be made in the morning or handouts to be placed in the school libraries.

FANDOM FRENZY

Whether it's superheroes, witches and wizards, hobbits, Janeites, Time Lords, or zombies—odds are there are many fanboys and fangirls who want to celebrate their love of their favorite pop culture book, TV show, or movie. The possibilities are endless for a fandom or comic con event that unites people over their shared interests. Celebrate one fandom or many at this event—librarian's choice. Encourage cosplay (costumes and makeup), make Harry Potter's butterbeer (or an alternative drink or snack), read bad fanfiction, debate the actions of the characters, and more.

PREPARATION TIME	LENGTH OF PROGRAM	NUMBER OF PATRONS	SUGGESTED AGE RANGE
2 hours	1 hour	15–30	Older Teens–30s

SHOPPING LIST

» Plastic spoons
» Plastic cups
» Plastic bowls
» Butterscotch topping
» Soda water

» Cream soda
» Caramel sauce
» Whipped cream
» Salt

» Paper
» Pencils or pens
» Movie soundtrack CDs
» Laptop

SETUP

2 Months Before
» Determine if you want to celebrate one fandom or multiples at this event and market accordingly.
» Research fandoms you are unfamiliar with and prepare your costume.

1 Week Before
» Purchase ingredients for butterbeer and gather supplies.
» Search for bad fanfiction on the Internet.
» Check out soundtracks or scores from the library of popular fandoms.

1 Hour Before
» Set out the ingredients for the butterbeer on a table.
» Pull books, graphic novels, and movies to have available, including lesser-known titles.

MAKE IT HAPPEN

» Play music CDs as people walk in. See if people can guess which movie or TV show the music is from. Ask people about their costumes and how they made them.

» Once everyone is settled, encourage people to talk about how they came to their fandom and why they enjoy it.

» Read bad fanfiction aloud—this always provides a laugh. Ask if anyone has ever written fanfiction before. It can't be as bad as what you just read!

» Take a break and make a snack or drink related to the fandom—in this case, butterbeer (see the directions at the end of this section).

» Readers' advisory: Offer favorites of yours and then ask theirs. Chances are participants will have a lot to suggest to others. Offer them the pulled graphic novels, books, and movies to check out.

» Introduction to LARPing (Live Action Role-Playing): If you have a particularly outgoing or gregarious group, encourage them to LARP. Participants role-play as characters in the novels or movies. This can be done as a game or you can pose questions, such as, How would characters from two different fandoms interact? In what world? What would happen if person A did this instead of that? There are also role-playing games available as board games or online to assist with this.

> **BUTTERBEER INSTRUCTIONS** (http://allrecipes.com/recipe/butterbeer-ii)
>
> 1. Combine butterscotch topping (2 tablespoons) and soda water (1 cup) in a plastic cup; stir until thoroughly mixed. Add the cream soda (1 cup) into the cup.
>
> 2. Stir whipped cream (2 tablespoons) and caramel sauce (2 tablespoons) together with a pinch of salt in a small bowl.
>
> 3. Spoon onto the soda mixture. Stir lightly; it will froth.

VARIATIONS

» Comic Con for All Ages: This program can be expanded into a library-wide, multi-hour family event, if desired. Hire a face painter and have an all-ages costume contest. Have a superhero mask–making activity. Bring in graphic novel authors and illustrators to present a panel discussion and to sell their books. Show a superhero-themed movie.

» Premiere Night: Kick off a favorite TV show or movie that you have a particular affinity for. Chances are if you love it, other people do, too. Have a viewing party at the library and serve snacks that correlate to the fandom.

» Older Teens: Celebrate the latest young adult book-to-movie release. Advertise trivia, favorite quotes, snacks, and movie tickets.

POWER PROMOTION

» This is a great program to coincide with Free Comic Book Day on the first Saturday in May.

» Ask comic book shops in your area to promote this event, participate, or hang flyers.

» If there is a movie currently playing that corresponds with your event, ask the theater manager to hang flyers or a poster.

THROWBACK HALLOWEEN NIGHT

This program combines many elements of the '80s and '90s Nights (see the April and May chapters) with an emphasis on celebrating Halloween like we did when we were kids!

PREPARATION TIME	LENGTH OF PROGRAM	NUMBER OF PATRONS	SUGGESTED AGE RANGE
3 hours shopping and setup	1½ hours	30	20s–30s

SHOPPING LIST

» Small pumpkins
» Acrylic paint
» Paintbrushes
» Glazed donuts
» Twine

» Chocolate pudding snack cups
» Oreos (original)
» Gummy worms
» Plastic spoons
» Paper plates

» Napkins
» Candy assortment (see suggestions under '80s Night in the April chapter and '90s Night in the May chapter)

SETUP

2 Months Before
» Create a shopping and supply list based on the elements you've chosen to include in your program.

1 Week Before
» Shop for supplies.

1 Hour Before
» Set up craft and treat stations.
» Cue up a movie or playlist if you're going to incorporate either one into the program.

MAKE IT HAPPEN

» Pumpkin painting: Carving pumpkins can be just a tad messy, so having participants paint small pumpkins is a fun alternative.
» DIY snacks: Have a station where participants can make their own dirt cups using the pudding snack cups, gummy worms, and crumbled Oreos.
» "Bobbing" for donuts: As a far more sanitary alternative to bobbing for apples, string up your glazed donuts using twine and hold a contest to see who among the participants can eat through his or hers the fastest. Award prizes to winners.

VARIATIONS

» Consider holding a best-dressed competition and award prizes to participants who are wearing the best Halloween costumes. (Make sure to advertise this competition in all of your program promotions so that attendees know to dress up!)
» Consider playing a spooky songs mix or showing a throwback spooky movie or TV show throughout the program. Old-school shows like *Goosebumps* and *Are You Afraid of the Dark?* are now available on DVD, so check whether your library has either one of those available. Having a series of 30-minute episodes of either of those classic television shows would make for nice background entertainment that participants can drop into and out of as they desire.

POWER PROMOTION

» Post flyers near your browsing AV collections such as CDs and DVDs. If possible, create a DVD display of popular '70s, '80s, and '90s horror or Halloween films and include on it information about the program.
» Reach out to local comic shops, game stores, and costume or party supply stores and ask to post flyers in their establishments.

11

NOVEMBER

PATRONS WILL BE thankful for library programs this month as they attend these offerings.

Recipe Scrapbooking helps young adults find ideas for gifts that are enjoyable and easy to put together. Many will appreciate the Holiday Spirit Winery Tour and Tasting.

Mystery fans will enjoy being in the cast for or attending the Mystery Dinner. And readers will enjoy learning about cupcake decorating and books about food at Delicious Reads. More creations can be inspired when the library celebrates NaNoWriMo this month by presenting a special program to encourage writers.

Creative and engaged patrons will find plenty to attract their interest at the library.

RECIPE SCRAPBOOKING

Recipe organization can be an ongoing struggle, no matter a person's cooking level. Emerging adults who are living on their own for the first time might find themselves inundated with recipes from helpful friends and family. This program is a low-key combination of crafting and organizing that also provides a great opportunity for socializing.

PREPARATION TIME	LENGTH OF PROGRAM	NUMBER OF PATRONS	SUGGESTED AGE RANGE
2½ hours shopping and setup	1½ hours	20	20s–30s

SHOPPING LIST

- » 3-ring binders (at least 1")
- » Page protectors (10–15 per binder, plus extras)
- » Card stock in various colors
- » Pens, markers
- » Glue sticks
- » Scissors
- » Food- and cooking-related scrapbooking decals, stickers

SETUP

1 Week Before
- » Shop for supplies.

1–2 Hours Before
- » Place page protectors in binders.
- » Set binders on supply table so that patrons can pick them up as they enter.
- » Place stacks of card stock as well as pens, markers, and glue sticks on supply table as well.

MAKE IT HAPPEN

» In advertising for your program, make sure to inform participants that they should be prepared to trim and glue their recipes. They should bring 8½" × 11" or smaller copies of any recipes that they don't want to alter.

» First, have participants group their recipes however they prefer (appetizers, breads, desserts, etc.) to assist them in laying out how they plan to organize their scrapbook.

» There is obviously no one way that participants have to organize their recipes, but you can present them with options and provide feedback.

» The main event consists of participants trimming their recipes however they see fit and gluing them to the card stock, which will then go into the page protectors in the binder.

» If they prefer, participants can create title pages and tables of contents for their scrapbooks as well.

VARIATIONS

» Organize and Swap: Turn your recipe scrapbooking program into a recipe swap as well (see Quick and Easy Recipe Swap in the July chapter).

POWER PROMOTION

» Reach out to local craft stores and ask to post flyers in those establishments.

» Create a book display that combines cookbooks with crafting books and put information about the program on it.

HOLIDAY SPIRIT
WINERY TOUR AND TASTING

Get in the holiday spirit while enjoying a tasting of holiday wines. Discover which wines go best with certain meals and desserts to help you decide what to bring to holiday celebrations. Although many people enjoy wine, they often stick with what they already know and enjoy. This is a chance to go out into the community and expand people's knowledge about different types of wine, what matches with particular foods, and the winemaking process.

PREPARATION TIME	LENGTH OF PROGRAM	NUMBER OF PATRONS	SUGGESTED AGE RANGE
1 hour setup	2 hours	15–30	21–40s

SHOPPING LIST

» Note cards
» Pencils

SETUP

2 Months Before
» Contact a local winery and arrange to have a tour and tasting.
» Ask to have the tasting related specifically to holiday treats or meals.
» If you do not have a winery in your area, consider hiring an instructor to come into the library for a holiday tasting event.

1 Week Before
» Ask the winery what wines will be served, what types of wines they are, their tastes (light, fruity, oaky, etc.), and what foods match well.
» Create a handout with that information for your patrons to take home.

1 Hour Before
» Gather supplies and meet patrons at the winery.

MAKE IT HAPPEN

» Welcome everyone and thank the winery for a great partnership.
» Hand out pencils and note cards if anyone is interested in taking notes.
» Explore the winery and learn about the winemaking process from the experts.
» Pass out the handout so that participants can add notes about the wines tasted.
» Participate in the tasting and learn about different types of wines.
» Ask opinions about the different types of wines tasted: What was their favorite? What would they pair this wine with?

VARIATIONS

» Make Your Own Wine: Purchase a winemaking kit or hire an instructor to teach a class about making wine. See the Craft Brewing program in the March chapter for similar ideas and instructions.
» A winery tour and tasting can be done almost any time throughout the year. Choose a season that works best for your library and winery.
» Older Teens: Sample holiday treats from around the world. Give background information about the history of each dessert. Serve with sparkling grape juice.

POWER PROMOTION

» Place flyers at the winery that is hosting the event.
» Promote this program at similar events: Craft Brewing, DIY Holiday Parties, and the like.
» Hang flyers at local wine bars and liquor stores.

MYSTERY DINNER

In *A Year of Programs for Teens 2,* Amy Alessio provided a sample mystery dinner outline with character sketches. The script was successfully performed with both adult staff and teen sets of characters at the Schaumburg Township District Library. With updated instructions, here is the script geared toward adults.

This style of mystery dinner requires at least one run-through ahead of time, but not elaborate hours of rehearsal. The script revolves around a pizza restaurant and works well when the library serves pizza to the audience while the mystery goes on.

PREPARATION TIME	LENGTH OF PROGRAM	NUMBER OF PATRONS	SUGGESTED AGE RANGE
5 hours, including rehearsal time	1½ hours	50, plus 8–11 volunteers for cast	20s–40s

SHOPPING LIST

- » Pizza for cast and audience
- » Drinks
- » Cookies, cupcakes, or ice cream novelties for dessert course
- » Paper goods for serving
- » Props for mystery (baggies, gloves, camera, bed sheet, fingerprint kit and tweezers for CSI techs, sign for door reading "Pizza Pete's Restaurant," partially used spray bottle of cleaning solution)
- » Costumes for mystery (all characters should dress for their parts with any props they feel they need—for example, the Detective could have a badge, a notebook, and a pen)
- » Prizes for the winning team and the most creative team (for example, mystery books, detective kits, or gift certificates for pizza)

SETUP

1 Month Before

- » Contact adult or staff volunteers and match them to parts. Most parts could be changed from man to woman or vice versa. Send cast members their own profile and the questions they will be asked, along with the time line for the evening.
- » Make a handout for the audience that includes a brief description of each character, along with space for notes. See the section on the Interrogation for more information on what audience members should know as opposed to cast members.
- » Make forms for players to turn in—one per table—about who did the murder and why.

2 Weeks Before

» Go over the entire evening with the cast. Some may need to review their "interrogation" a few times. This should not take more than 90 minutes.

2 Hours Before

» Set up the room and order pizzas.
» Cast should be in place a half hour before the program begins.

MAKE IT HAPPEN

Characters

» Pizza Pete Pastachio
» CSI techs—up to three
» Paul Pastachio
» Phil Pastachio
» Kurt Hartake

» Edwina Moolah
» Louise Luvacuccio
» Margot Glamore
» Olive Sparkle
» Detective

Props

» Sign for door indicating that the room is Pizza Pete's Restaurant
» Room should be set up like a restaurant with tables and chairs
» Table at front for "interrogations"

SETUP

» Kurt greets guests as they come in and helps to seat them. He will then serve pizza from the kitchen to the three Pastachio brothers and Louise, who will be sitting at the front of the room.
» Olive is cleaning up in the kitchen, where people can see her.
» Edwina is walking around muttering, angry.
» Margot is walking around furtively.
» Guests should come in and eat pizza and have their drinks. On their tables are pencils, the overviews of all cast members (including Pizza Pete, as he will not yet be dead), and forms to fill out about who killed the victim and why.

Action (when most of the audience has arrived)

» Pizza Pete is enjoying a nice dinner with friends when suddenly he screams, clutches at his throat, and falls to the floor.
» Staff call 911, and police and three crime scene techs arrive and take over. (This is an optional way to use extra volunteers if available.) They discuss the body, take fingerprints with the CSI kit, pick up things with tweezers, use chemicals, and then throw a sheet over the body. They also take pictures. They pick up the pepperoni and put it into baggies. Then they leave and come back to talk with the Detective in a way that everyone can hear. They are concerned because

they cannot find the cleaning solution that was likely used for the crime anywhere, though they feel some of it was dumped on a plant that is dying behind the restaurant. They found shards of plastic in the now jammed incinerator.

Intermission

» This is a great time to serve dessert or let guests go through an ice cream sundae bar so that Pizza Pete can be removed from the scene.
» Pizza Pete is carried out (or subtlety sneaks out) of the room at this point.
» The Detective announces that there has been a murder and that no one is to leave.

Action

» The Detective begins to "interrogate" suspects. He calls up each "suspect" and asks questions based on each one's profile. Then the characters circulate among the tables, while the guests ask them questions. The guests will be eating their dessert, and then they have a few minutes to decide who the killer is before turning in their forms. The first team to turn in a form with the correct answers wins.

Interrogation Information for Cast

The following information should be given to all cast members ahead of time for rehearsals. It contains everything they need to know about their characters as well as the questions to be asked by the Detective during the show.

The audience may be given a form with a list of characters and a couple of sentences about each, enough to introduce each person and keep the characters straight but not enough to give away the plot.

» PIZZA PETE PASTACHIO is/was a famous pizza chef at a restaurant in [Your Town]. Although the dead man will not be interrogated, this information can be used by all the rest of the "suspects." Pete has written a best-selling cookbook. He has two brothers who run a famous restaurant in Venice, Italy, and Pete claims his pizza recipes are from there. He has a heavy gambling habit and plans on soon taking his money and going to the Bahamas, where he will become a professional gambler.
» LOUISE LUVACUCCIO: A former computer tech in a big corporation, Louise wants to become a chef and works long shifts in Pete's restaurant as a waitress. They have dated for three years and repeatedly avoid talking about marriage. She developed many of the "award-winning recipes" but is painfully shy and has been happy to let Pete take the credit, until recently. She has spent many afternoons weeping on Kurt's shoulder. She found out about the girlfriend this morning. She heard the argument with Edwina and realized the money was going to the girlfriend. She saw a bottle of cleaning solution and sprayed it on the pepperoni pizza slice before serving it. Then she felt bad and decided to eat the pepperoni pizza slice to kill herself dramatically in front of Pete. She switched the plates just

before they were served in the kitchen, setting them up so she would receive the poisoned pepperoni pizza slice. She went to the bathroom to get her nerve up, and to erase the evidence of her crying, then went out to join the brothers for dinner.

Name?

Occupation? You also did some cooking?

What was your relationship with Pete?

I've heard you were his fiancée. How did you feel about that?

What time did you come in?

What did you do when you came in? Did you do any cleaning? Was there anyone else in the kitchen?

You ate with Pete and his two brothers? What time?

What did you talk about?

Who served the pizza?

You didn't put anything in the pizza, did you?

You overheard the argument between Pete and Edwina Moolah, didn't you?

What were they arguing about?

I understand that Pete was seeing Margot Glamore?

Were you aware of Kurt's interest in you?

Did you use the cleaning solution? Did you put it on the pizza?

» **PHIL PASTACHIO AND PAUL PASTACHIO** are Pete's brothers from Italy. They speak limited English and converse in (phony) Italian or broken phrases before responding to each question from the Detective. They especially cannot understand any questions about where their family money comes from. In fact, their restaurant is not doing well since their mother became ill and no longer cooks for them. Their mother was an infamous assassin in Italy as well. They came here hoping to steal Pete's new "recipes" and use them in the family restaurant in Italy.

Names?

What was your relationship with Pete?

What was your role in Pete's restaurant? What were you discussing with Pete when he died?

What was the last thing Pete said to you?

What time did you arrive?

Why are you here in America?

Mother's restaurant? Why didn't your mother come with you? Your mother is under investigation by Interpol? Word is that your mother is a hit man for the Mafia. Is that right? She doesn't put things in the pizza that don't belong there, does she?

How did you feel about Pete's death?

» **EDWINA MOOLAH** is the banker who gave the money to Pizza Pete for his restaurant. She knew the Pastachios in Italy and gave Pete the money after she tasted Louise's pizza. Pete recently asked for more money to "expand his business." Edwina gave him an undocumented loan and kept the interest herself. Pete recently found this out when he visited the bank to make an extra payment, and he had an argument with Edwina before tonight's dinner.

Name?

Occupation?

What was your relationship with Pete?

What time did you arrive? What did you do between the time you arrived and the time Pete died?

Why were you here tonight?

Had an argument with Pete?

Checking financial records revealed some irregularities. High interest? The bank charges that high of an interest? You loaned him your own money, not the bank's?

» KURT HARTAKE is the host at the restaurant and a medical student. Kurt is the killer, and this character needs to be cagey while avoiding discussing the following information: He is in love with Louise and switched the pizza slices after watching her spray the slice and then serve it to herself. He thought she made a mistake serving it to herself, and he made sure Pete ate it instead. Then he dumped the cleaning solution in a plant behind the restaurant and put the bottle in the incinerator, after wiping it down. Kurt saw Louise in the kitchen when he took his smoking break, then came in to switch the plates. Then he went to his post at the door.

Name?

Occupation? Medical student?

What was your relationship with Pete?

What time did you arrive?

What did you do after you arrived? Did you see anybody else in the kitchen?

You served the pizza? Did you serve individual slices?
Was there anybody in the kitchen when you left?

What was your relationship with Louise Luvacuccio? You seem more interested in Louise than just as a coworker.

Who usually does the cleaning in the kitchen?

Did you know about Pete's other girlfriend?

Did their relationship bother you?

» MARGOT GLAMORE is the Internet girlfriend who has been dating Pete online through the library computers. Pete is not her only boyfriend; in fact, she solicits men from all over, and they give her money, plane tickets, anything—then she disappears. She met Pete in person a month ago and told him she needed money to leave her current boyfriend who was beating her. Pete gave her a plane ticket to the Bahamas. She really likes Pete and came to the restaurant tonight to reimburse him for the ticket.

Name?
_____

Occupation? Unemployed?
_____

What was your relationship with Pete? How long?
_____

Did you have other relationships with men you met on the Internet? They gave you gifts? Money?
_____

Did you know that Pete was already seeing Louise Luvacuccio?
_____

How did you feel about that?
_____

Why did you come to visit Pete at this time?
_____

What did Pete give you money for?
_____

Checking financial records revealed two one-way tickets to the Bahamas.
_____

» OLIVE SPARKLE is the head of the cleaning staff for the restaurant. She takes her job very, very seriously. She was upset when she couldn't find her cleaning solution tonight as she noticed a thumbprint on the door. She went to find the solution around 6:10. She had not seen it since 5:30, when she was cleaning the mirrors in the washroom. Her Italian grandmother was killed by the brothers' mother, and Olive has not yet figured out what she wants to do for revenge.

Name?
_____

Occupation?
_____

What was your relationship with Pete? Good boss?
_____

What time did you arrive?
_____

What did you do after you arrived? Cleaning solution? Mirrors?

Where were you when Pete died?

Grandmother? Trouble between your family and the Pastachios?

After the Interrogation

» Consider offering an ice cream bar after the interrogation while inviting cast members to circulate once more. Audience members should have all the information they need from the interrogation, and this second interview with the cast members is not necessary, but it heightens the drama and lengthens the time. Be sure to mark the time each form is turned in from audience members with the name of the killer and the reason.

» After the forms have been turned in, have the Detective go over all the wrong answers first, asking the wrong cast members if they did it. They will deny it. When the Detective gets to Kurt, Kurt should proclaim that he did it to save Louise. He is "arrested" by the Detective and led out. Award prizes for the winning team and the most creative team before the program ends.

VARIATIONS

» This program can be done without serving the audience pizza. It can also be done as a fund-raiser by charging money at the door or selling tickets in advance or as an Older Teens program. At the Schaumburg Township District Library, it was done as a staff program by staff for staff, with monies donated at the door going to charity after the cost of the food was covered.

POWER PROMOTION

» Do not make posters indicating "murder in the library." Rather, invite participants to an evening at Pizza Pete's, where they may be needed to solve a crime among a cast of suspects.

» Create a display of mystery books with cutout footprints leading adults from another department, where program information would also be featured.

» Make sample "badges" with program information on them to hand out at events during the month before this program, indicating that recipients are "deputized" to come and help solve the case.

DELICIOUS READS

Heading into the holidays, many people are looking for new recipes and reads. Combine these interests with a food book–themed event. Invite patrons to bring in thirty copies of their favorite recipes to exchange.

PREPARATION TIME	LENGTH OF PROGRAM	NUMBER OF PATRONS	SUGGESTED AGE RANGE
2 hours shopping and setup	1½ hours	30	30s–40s

SHOPPING LIST

» Plain cupcakes or cookies to decorate, enough for each attendee to make at least two
» Napkins
» Small plates
» Toothpicks
» Plastic knives

» Waxed paper
» Scissors
» Frosting in pressurized cans with attached tips (the kind that is sprayed on like Cheez Whiz or whipped cream)

Houndstooth Frosting
» White frosting
» Tubes of colored gel (3–4 tubes should be enough)

Tie-Dye
» White frosting
» Tubes of colored gel (3 more tubes should be enough for participants to try this one as well)

Stencil Frosting
» Colored frosting
» Colored sugar

Snowballs
» White frosting
» Shredded coconut

Fancy Tips
» Water and cups (optional)

SETUP

1 Month Before

» Compare the accompanying book list with the library collection and substitute titles or order as needed. Make notes to booktalk as desired.

» Practice the cupcake decorating techniques if they are new to you. Take photos and make slides or short movies of the techniques, if desired. (Or find movies and links with instructions online to show patrons at the event.)

» Make a handout with the book titles and decorating ideas.

1 Week Before

» Shop for as much as possible, though cookies and cupcakes are freshest closer to the program.

» Make a display with the books, though some may need to be kept to show at the program.

1 Hour Before

» Chairs should be set up around tables that are within view of the speaker.

» Set up the decorating stations with supplies for each technique. Some will require some prep, such as cutting small, waxed-paper squares for the stencil table.

MAKE IT HAPPEN

» As patrons come in, invite them to sit at a table.

» When most patrons have arrived, give a 30- to 40-minute booktalk on the food titles.

» Demonstrate, either with PowerPoint or live, how to do each technique for cupcake decorating. Instruct patrons to choose two techniques.

» Houndstooth Frosting: For this method, frost the cupcake or cookie smoothly on top. Make a few parallel lines with the gel tubes, and use a toothpick to pull perpendicular lines through the gel, forming a loose grid for the houndstooth effect.

» Tie-Dye: Frost the cupcake or cookie smoothly. Make three or four rings of gel from the center out. Use a toothpick to make radial lines from the center out, creating a tie-dye effect.

» Stencil Frosting: Cut one simple shape out of the center of a precut 3" to 4" square of waxed paper (for example, a heart). The squares may vary in size according to how large the cupcakes or cookies are. Frost the cupcake or cookie smoothly, then place the stencil lightly on the frosting. Sprinkle colored sugar inside the shape, making a neat image.

» Snowballs: Peel the paper off the cupcakes, if needed. If cookies are used, stack a few small ones to create the snowball effect. Frost the outside of the cupcake or stack all the way around—sides, bottom, everything. Then sprinkle coconut liberally, making a snowball.

FANCY TIPS Invite program attendees to practice making little flowers or roses on scraps of waxed paper, using the different tips that come with the pressurized cans of frosting. Then participants can cover their cupcake or cookie with the flowers.

VARIATIONS

» Sweet Treats and Reads: Offer this event in February, with mostly romance-themed books.
» Cupcake Crazy: Offer the cupcake decorating as a program without the books.
» Read 'Em and Eat: Offer snacks and treats for patrons to enjoy while hearing about the books.

POWER PROMOTION

» Food programs usually do not need extra advertising, but a display of books from the book list or about cake decorating will attract extra attention. Bookmarks about the event placed in each book will help patrons remember the event.

DELICIOUS READS BOOK LIST

The first title in a series is listed unless another was featured for the theme. Subtitles are omitted from this list, making it easily transferable to a PowerPoint presentation that would include basic text and book covers.

Authors with Cookbooks
» *Debbie Macomber's Christmas Cookbook*
» *Joanne Fluke's Lake Eden Cookbook*
» *Sneaky Pie's Cookbook for Mystery Lovers*

Book Lovers' Cookbooks
» Gelman, Judy. *The Book Club Cookbook*
» Grossman, Jo. *A Taste of Murder*

Famous Fictional Characters
» Davis, Robin. *The Star Wars Cookbook*
» Bucholz, Dinah. *The Unofficial Harry Potter Cookbook*

Famous Chef in Literature
» Powell, Julie. *Julie & Julia*

A Famous Chef's Position
» Hyzy, Julie. *State of the Onion*

When Food Steals the Scene
» Stockett, Kathryn. *The Help*
» Karon, Jan. *At Home in Mitford*
» Flagg, Fannie. *Fried Green Tomatoes at the Whistle Stop Café*

Food Fiction Flavors All Senses
» Esquival, Laura. *Like Water for Chocolate*

Parodies of Famous Fiction
» Fowler, F. L. *Fifty Shades of Chicken*

Farm Fresh and Food Trucks
» Haywood, B. B. *Town in a Blueberry Jam*
» Pike, Penny. *Death of a Crabby Cook*
» Shelton, Paige. *Farm Fresh Murder*
» Connolly, Sheila. *One Bad Apple*

Drinks?
» Landis, Jill Marie. *Mai Tai One On*
» Coyle, Cleo. *On What Grounds*

Solid Chocolate
» Roberts, Sheila. *Better Than Chocolate*
» Carl, Joanna. *The Chocolate Cat Caper*

Cookie Crumbling
» Fluke, Joanne. *Chocolate Chip Cookie Murder*
» Lowells, Virginia. *Cookie Dough or Die*

Wedding Cakes = Romance
» Mallery, Susan. *Falling for Gracie*
» Roberts, Nora. *Savor the Moment*

Inspirational Cakes
» Byrd, Sandra. *Let Them Eat Cake*
» Hinton, Lynne. *Friendship Cake*
» Clipston, Amy. *Gift of Grace*

Cupcakes—From Sweet to Spicy?
» McKinlay, Jenn. *Sprinkle with Murder*
» Kauffman, Donna. *Sugar Rush*

Baking Magic
» Cates, Bailey. *Brownies and Broomsticks*
» Jaffarian, Sue Ann. *Ghost à la Mode*

Preponderance of Pie
» Adams, Ellery. *Pies and Prejudice*
» Culver, Carol. *A Good Day to Pie*

Even Doughnuts
» Beck, Jessica. *Glazed for Murder*

Southern Cuisine
» Herbert, A. L. *Murder with Fried Chicken and Waffles*
» Shelton, Paige. *If Fried Chicken Could Fly*
» Davis, Krista. *The Diva Runs Out of Thyme*

Pennsylvania Dutch
» Myers, Tamar. *Too Many Crooks Spoil the Broth*

International Cuisine
» Campion, Alexander. *The Grave Gourmet*

Middle Eastern Cuisine
» Mehran, Marsha. *Pomegranate Soup*

Paranormal, Crafts, and Food
» MacRae, Molly. *Last Wool and Testament*

More Crafting with Food
» Chiaverini, Jennifer. *The New Year's Quilt*

Tea, Scrapbooking, and Food
» Childs, Laura. *Death by Darjeeling*
» Childs, Laura. *Keepsake Crimes*
» Childs, Laura. *Eggs in Purgatory*

Pizza and Restaurant Mysteries
» Cavender, Chris. *A Slice of Murder*
» Rosen, Delia. *A Brisket, a Casket*
» Page, Katherine Hall. *The Body in the Boudoir*
» Davidson, Diane Mott. *Catering to Nobody*

Holiday Food Titles
» Meier, Leslie. *Mistletoe Murder*
» Washburn, Livia J. *The Gingerbread Bump-Off*

Caterers, Critics, Collectors
» Crawford, Isis. *A Catered Murder*
» Burdette, Lucy. *An Appetite for Murder*
» Hamilton, Victoria. *A Deadly Grind*

Food Fusion: Romance
» Edwards, Louisa. *Too Hot to Touch*

Make That Hot—Not Haute
» Usen, Amanda. *Scrumptious*

Romantic Italian Cooking
» Senate, Melissa. *The Love Goddess' Cooking School*

Women's Fiction
» O'Neal, Barbara. *How to Bake a Perfect Life*
» Ballis, Stacey. *Recipe for Disaster*

HUNGRY FOR MORE? RESOURCES

Food Mysteries: http://literaryfoodie.blogspot.com/p/food-mysteries-list.html

Popular Food Mysteries Books: www.goodreads.com/shelf/show/food-mysteries

The Cozy Mystery List Blog: www.cozy-mystery.com/blog/cozy-mystery-authors-with-culinary -themes-part-2.html

Fiction with Recipes: http://publiclibrary.cc/readalikes/fiction%20with%20recipes.htm

NaNoWriMo KICKOFF AND WEEKLY WRITE-INS

National Novel Writing Month (NaNoWriMo) takes place each November and encourages writers to knock out a 50,000-word manuscript during the month. It's an intense time for those participating, and it's a great opportunity to foster patrons' creative endeavors with space, snacks, and helpful hints.

PREPARATION TIME	LENGTH OF PROGRAM	NUMBER OF PATRONS	SUGGESTED AGE RANGE
1½ hours shopping and setup	2+ hours	25	Teens and 20s

SHOPPING LIST

» Snacks (coffee, tea, water, cookies, chips, and candy or chocolate are always popular)

SETUP

1 Week Before
» Shop for supplies.
» Create writing prompts to scatter throughout the room for people who need a boost while writing.

1 Hour Before
» Set up a beverage and snack table.
» Consider including books from your library's collection that discuss writing and the writing process as well as how to get published.

MAKE IT HAPPEN

» The key aspect of this program is giving participants a space to work on their writing projects. Make sure you have plenty of tables and chairs at which participants can sit, and set up a table with snacks and beverages.
» You can also provide writing prompts on 3" × 5" note cards to help participants combat any writer's block and stir their imaginations. Writing prompts can be as simple as random words and phrases, or you can provide questions for writers to try to answer within their stories.

VARIATIONS

» The number of write-ins you do throughout the month is up to you and might depend on how many patrons are interested in the program. If you think you'll have a large turnout, you could do a kickoff program during the first week of the month, weekly write-ins throughout the month, and a completion celebration during the first week of December (you won't want to have the completion celebration during the last week of November—people will still be writing!).

» Encourage—but don't require—participants to share what they are working on with their peers in the group. Some people might be eager for feedback, while others will prefer to keep to themselves and work on their pieces.

POWER PROMOTION

» If your library sponsors any writing clubs, or if writing clubs use your space for meetings, be sure to reach out to them and invite them to the program. They can also help spread the word to fellow writers outside the library.

» Chances are there might be some writers among your book club participants as well, so be sure to advertise the program during book club meetings.

» In addition to the ways you typically advertise your programs, consider posting information near your library's books on writing and self-publishing.

DECEMBER

ALTHOUGH YOUNG CHILDREN can't wait for the holidays, adults usually have some wariness mixed in with the anticipation.

Help adults ease the pressure of the holiday season with DIY Holiday Parties and DIY Holiday Gifts and Decorations on the Cheap.

If parents and young adults are looking for something fun to do during vacation days, a Museum Fair will remind them about special local offerings.

And writers who finished NaNoWriMo or who want to start the next year with a bang can enjoy Smart Tips for Self-Publishing.

Finish out the year with popular and realistic event variations for every library.

DIY HOLIDAY PARTIES

The holidays are a stressful and costly time for many folks, but holiday parties don't have to break the bank for the host or hostess. There are many creative solutions to organizing a cost-effective holiday party: games, crafting the perfect centerpiece, snacks, music, cookie decorating, and a recipe exchange, to name a few. Celebrate the end of the year (and surviving a year of Millennial programs and beyond) with a holiday party and a DIY workshop.

PREPARATION TIME	LENGTH OF PROGRAM	NUMBER OF PATRONS	SUGGESTED AGE RANGE
2–3 hours	2 hours	30–40	20s–30s

SHOPPING LIST

- » Name tags
- » Note cards or recipe cards
- » Board games
- » Pens
- » Sugar cookies
- » Gingerbread men
- » Gel tubes with decorating tips
- » Frosting
- » Plastic knives
- » Paper plates
- » Paper cups
- » Napkins
- » Bottled water
- » Eggnog
- » Karaoke machine or computer
- » Microphone
- » Holiday CDs
- » Trivia prizes
- » Christmas lights
- » Tape
- » Pinecones
- » Ribbon
- » Glitter
- » Glue
- » Candles
- » Ornaments
- » Fake cranberries
- » Glass cylinders or mason jars

SETUP

2 Months Before

- » When creating the program description, include asking people to bring in their favorite, simple recipes and a white elephant present (a wrapped gift from home that is often silly, random, and of minimal value).
- » Determine what type of craft and centerpiece you want to create.
- » Choose materials that are cheap, can easily be found in homes or craft stores, and are adaptable to other projects. This is a great opportunity to clean out your craft closet or use ideas from the DIY Holiday Gifts and Decorations on the cheap program.

1 Week Before

» Purchase crafting and food (nonperishable) supplies for your various stations and prizes for trivia winners.

» Create a time line for your program.

» Make a holiday trivia handout and print copies with answers to give to people to use at their own parties. Include holiday trivia from around the world and use answer sheets from the Trivia Nights programs (see the Clubs That Keep Them Coming Back chapter). On the other side of the handout include the DIY ideas used at this program as well as ideas that aren't feasible at the library (for example, having a snowball fight or decorating a tree).

1–2 Hours Before

» Borrow board games from Teen and Youth Services staff.

» Set up different stations of activities: recipe exchange, centerpiece crafting, cookie decorating, karaoke, games, and trivia.

» Hang Christmas lights on the wall as a backdrop and encourage people to take photos and upload them to social media.

MAKE IT HAPPEN

» Ask people to sign in, put on a name tag, and place their white elephant gift in a designated area.

» Invite people to socialize and have free time: play board games, exchange recipes, craft, karaoke, and decorate cookies.

» Centerpiece craft: Provide a decorated centerpiece made in a glass cylinder or mason jar—any dish will work. Invite participants to use fake cranberries, pinecones, candles, glitter, and ornaments to create unique centerpieces for their own homes.

» Trivia: Ask fifteen to twenty holiday-themed questions and offer prizes to the winning team or individual.

» White elephant exchange: Ask attendees to sit in a circle with presents in the middle. The first person can choose a present, and the second person can steal it or choose another. Continue around the circle. There are multiple ways to play this game.

» Gingerbread men cookie decorating: Invite patrons to use the gels and tips to decorate gingerbread men.

» Pass out the trivia and DIY handout that offers additional suggestions that may not have been feasible at the library, such as a mulled wine or glögg spicing contest, decorating a tree, bad Christmas movie lip reading, a snowball fight, and the like.

VARIATIONS

» Formal Parties: Learn the etiquette of hosting a formal dinner party—how to fold napkins into fancy shapes, how to arrange silverware, types of food to be served, and so forth.
» Older Teens: Put a spin on traditional gingerbread houses and create haunted gingerbread houses out of oatmeal or Pop-Tarts boxes. Use graham crackers, dark colored frosting, and candy decorations, such as M&Ms, candy corn, mini marshmallows, licorice, and the like. Just make sure that more candy goes on the haunted gingerbread houses than in the teens' mouths.

POWER PROMOTION

» With permission of the establishments, post flyers at holiday stores, Christmas tree lots, and crafting stores.
» Encourage attendees at other Millennials programs to come; this is a celebration for them as well as a DIY program.
» Create a display of holiday-themed books, CDs, or DVDs and hang posters and flyers promoting the event.

DIY HOLIDAY GIFTS AND DECORATIONS ON THE CHEAP

The Big-Ass Book of Crafts by Mark Montano is one of many crafting manuals designed for younger adults, with fast and easy projects that still look great. Although expecting patrons to learn new techniques and have perfect projects in one 90-minute program is ambitious, this event will offer enough fun and easy techniques that all participants should finish a couple of things and have many ideas for more.

PREPARATION TIME	LENGTH OF PROGRAM	NUMBER OF PATRONS	SUGGESTED AGE RANGE
3 hours shopping and setup	1½–2 hours	25	20s–30s

SHOPPING LIST

Because of the number of supplies needed for this event, it may be helpful to ask for $5 at registration.

- » Scissors (both fancy-bladed scrapbooking [sold in inexpensive tubs] and straight for fabrics or ribbons)
- » Recycled plastic bags (for projects)
- » Baggies (for small projects, like bookmarks or beaded earrings)
- » Inexpensive table coverings

Quilled Bookmark
- » Card stock in a variety of bright or metallic shades
- » Quilling paper (tiny ¼" or ⅛" strips, found online or in craft stores)
- » Knitting needles or toothpicks
- » Glue sticks

Appetizer Tree
- » Toothpicks (optional)
- » Glue sticks
- » Foil in a variety of colors
- » Spools of velvet or other festive ribbons and rickrack
- » Straight pins
- » Styrofoam cones (large enough to hold about 60 toothpicks with fruit, cheese, or vegetables)

Beaded Earrings

» Strings of small beads (each set of earrings contains only a few)
» Tiny beads (one package, to begin and end earrings)
» Earring hardware (big value bags are available; the clip-on kind with attached, folding backs are efficient)
» Needle-nose pliers
» Wire cutters
» Surgical clamps (optional; helpful for holding and tightening jewelry findings)
» T-pins

Fringed Placemats

» Woven cloth in holiday or checkered fabrics (four 18" × 24" rectangles per person)
» Craft glue
» Spools of trim (about 1 per project)

Dried Rosebud Ball (for scent year-round or as an ornament)

» Dried rosebuds
» Craft glue (bottled works better than hot glue here)
» Small Styrofoam balls
» ⅛" ribbon in a variety of colors
» Straight pins (1 per project for bow and loop)

SETUP

2 Months Before

» Begin sourcing and collecting supplies and instructions for all projects and making samples.

1–2 Weeks Before

» Display samples and crafting books.
» Double-check all supplies.

1 Hour Before

» Cover tables.
» Set up each station with instructions, supplies, and tools.

MAKE IT HAPPEN

» As patrons arrive, direct them to a station.
» Everyone should have time to make at least three things, but do not police this rigidly. Someone may really enjoy making one craft and want to make several of it. Having some extra supplies on hand helps ease this situation. Another way is to ask if everyone has chosen three projects, and if so, participants are welcome to make extras of anything they want.
» Demonstrate each craft when everyone has arrived.
» Have half-sheet handouts with lists of supplies and instructions at each table in case patrons need to refer to them or want to know how to make more crafts than the program allows time for.

Quilled Bookmark

» Have patrons cut bookmarks with fancy scrapbooking scissors out of card stock.
» Show patrons how to wrap quilling paper around toothpicks or knitting needles. The shapes can be glued (using glue sticks) onto the top of the bookmark, so the flat, undecorated part remains in the book.
» The web page "Basics of Quilling" (www.auntannie.com/DecorativeCrafts/ Quilling) is a good site for learning beginning quilling techniques, including how to glue shapes onto the top of the bookmark.
» The North American Quilling Guild (www.naqg.org) is a great resource.

Appetizer Tree

» Show patrons how to cover Styrofoam cones with foil, securing it with straight pins. They can then wind ribbons or rickrack around the tree for decoration, also securing with a couple of pins.
» Patrons can then make a bow for the top, and the cone is ready to become an appetizer tree at parties.

Beaded Earrings

» If you are unfamiliar with putting these earrings together, keep a YouTube video handy on a laptop during the event, but these are pretty easy.
» Patrons put beads on T-pins, which are then attached to the backing hardware by winding the wire in a loop (using the needle-nose pliers) and then threading the loop through the hardware and cutting with the wire cutters.

Fringed Placemats

» Patrons glue a narrow trim as a border ½" to ¾" from the edges of each fabric rectangle. When the glue has dried, they gently pull threads up to that border to make a nice fringed effect.

Dried Rosebud Ball

» Patrons cover half the surface of a Styrofoam ball liberally with craft glue.
» They then stick dried rosebuds into the ball, through the glue, until the surface is covered.
» Patrons next put glue on the other half of the ball and insert rosebuds while gently holding on to the covered part. When the ball is completely covered, they should let it dry.
» When the ball is dry, they make a loop and bow with the thin ribbons and stick it in with a straight pin.

VARIATIONS

» Retro Holiday Crafts: Make any project listed for the Retro Craft Club (in the Clubs That Keep Them Coming Back chapter) with holiday-themed materials and turn them into simple gifts. For example, a pom-pom with three long pieces of yarn can have a braided tail and be a bookmark. Members of that club may want to help patrons in this program with projects, and new members could be recruited from this program.
» Older Teens: Teens have their own spin on projects and may enjoy working in a group by themselves with people their own age.

POWER PROMOTION

» Putting samples of projects with craft books on display, along with information about the program, is a great advertising technique. It will help assure those afraid of new crafting techniques that these projects will indeed be fast and easy. It will also show seasoned crafters that they may find some new ideas here in a low-pressure situation.
» Put photos of samples on bulletin boards with program information.
» Local craft suppliers may offer a discount on supplies if you promote their stores. They may also agree to advertise the event in their stores.

MUSEUM FAIR

Museums and libraries go hand in hand as learning and cultural centers. How can patrons tell which is the right museum for them and what types of collections and exhibits it has to offer? Is it appropriate for a 3-year-old, a 13-year-old, or a 33-year-old? At a Museum Fair, patrons can explore different museums, discover new ones they may not have heard of, and determine the best option for themselves or their family.

PREPARATION TIME	LENGTH OF PROGRAM	NUMBER OF PATRONS	SUGGESTED AGE RANGE
1–2 hours	1 hour	10–40	30s–40s

SHOPPING LIST

» Coffee
» Paper cups

» Pencils
» Video chat software (free)

SETUP

2 Months Before
» Create a presentation highlighting museums that are nearby. Include the type of museum, a brief overview, prices, special exhibits, age appropriateness, and so on.
» Contact nearby museums and ask if a representative can do a 10- to 15-minute virtual tour or speak at the library.
» Make sure to include a variety of museums and smaller, lesser-known museums.
» Download video chat software and test it.

1 Week Before
» Test video chat software with virtual presenters.
» Compile the presentation into a handout for patrons to write notes on and take home.

1 Hour Before
» Set up the video chat software and presentation system.
» Make sure virtual presenters are ready at their designated time.

MAKE IT HAPPEN

» Greet patrons and summarize which museums they'll be learning about today.
» Give information about the museums that were unable to send representatives or video chat.
» Introduce the presenters as you switch between video chats.
» Ask presenters about unique aspects of their museum and exhibits. What makes their museum different than others?
» Thank the museums and presenters. Ask the audience what was most helpful in this session and what museums they plan to go to.

VARIATIONS

» Behind the Scenes: Coordinate with a museum archivist or curator to go behind the scenes of exhibits or archives. An online alternative is to use a video chat to explore these areas with the help of a museum guide or archivist. With permission, stream or record this for later viewing on the library's website.
» Online: Explore museums or special exhibits from around the world. Many museums have online tours on their websites, so a video chat may not be necessary, but it would be an attendance draw if it could be arranged.
» Parents: Bring in a special collection from a museum exhibit (for example, dinosaur fossils or moon rocks). Coordinate with Youth Services for this program.

POWER PROMOTION

» Ask the museums if they will donate tickets or offer a discount for patrons who attend the program.
» Advertise this program at local preschools and elementary schools. Target young parents who may not be familiar with the area.
» Coordinate a display with loaned exhibit items from one or more of the museums. Advertise the Museum Fair in the display cases.

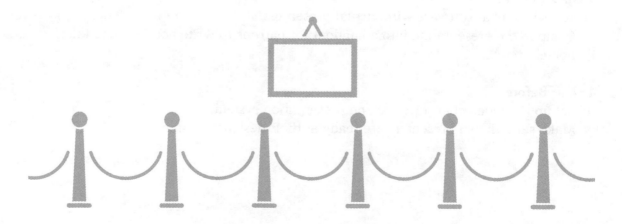

SMART TIPS FOR SELF-PUBLISHING

In December, many writers are looking at their projects from the past year and planning conferences and contests for the next year. Those who have finished a project may be thinking about self-publishing. Those who already self-publish may want to punch up their marketing or hire some professionals to help with one aspect of what is really a business. This program quickly runs over the basics of the entire process and offers tips on things to do—and things to avoid—in this quickly changing industry.

PREPARATION TIME	LENGTH OF PROGRAM	NUMBER OF PATRONS	SUGGESTED AGE RANGE
2 hours	1½ hours	40	20s–40s and beyond

SHOPPING LIST

» Raffle prizes for attendees, if desired (such as advance reader copies [ARCs], pens, mini journals, leftover summer reading prizes)
» Gifts for any guest speakers, if desired
» Index cards or scrap paper
» Pencils or pens

SETUP

2 Months Before
» Double-check the links on the accompanying handout (at the end of this program outline).
» Talk to the people in library writing groups or who participated in the November NaNoWriMo event and invite them to attend and share tips they have for their work as well.
» Speakers who have gone through the process are invaluable to the audience. Plan to have at least a couple of speakers offer tips.

1 Week Before
» Remind anyone who seemed interested in sharing tips from the writing groups that you approached.
» Research some current encouraging statistics about self-publishing to share with the audience.
» Pull some photos of popular self-published authors' work and covers.

1 Hour Before

» Double-check the AV equipment, especially the Internet connection. It may be a good idea to open links from the Resources section of this program description to share.

MAKE IT HAPPEN

» As people arrive, offer cards or scrap paper and pencils or pens for questions they may think of throughout the program along with the handouts so that they can make notes.
» Share some statistics, such as the number of books self-published on Amazon during recent months, or information about authors who have done very well, such as C. J. Lyons, J. A. Konrath, and Amanda Hocking. Amazon at times publishes information on self-publishing millionaires. Several have published all of their work online, whereas some had previous work published in print.
» Go through the budget, time line, marketing plan, and resources from the accompanying handout with the audience and invite them to make a loose plan from those categories for their project.
» Ask the audience about their favorite social media and what authors they may admire or follow already who do self-publishing.
» Show successful authors' covers and discuss positive features.
» Remind the audience of the groups or classes the library has available at which patrons can learn about social media, basic graphic design, or writing techniques.
» Invite audience members to discuss their experiences.
» Open the floor for questions. If a patron has a question about publishing memoirs, find that category in Amazon and show the best sellers so that the patron can get an idea of where to go for research. Other questions can be addressed in a similar fashion.

VARIATIONS

» Professional Speakers: Hire a freelance editor or self-published author to present the workshop.
» Online: Post the handout on a social media site such as Twitter and ask for other favorite resources or offer the handout in sections as an online class.
» Older Teens: Offer the same class, but focus on successful teen authors, such as Amanda Hocking. Discuss e-readers and how teens use social media before helping them draft a plan to market their work to other teens if that is what they are writing.

POWER PROMOTION

» Other than talking with the writing groups and NaNoWriMo participants, the best place to advertise this workshop is online, through the library website or social media.
» If the next issues of the *Writer's Guides* or new books for writers have recently arrived with information about publishing in the coming calendar year, display those with bookmarks containing information about the program.

HANDOUT/PROGRAM OUTLINE

Business Plan
» Hours available per week for this project
» Budget
» Content editing
» Copyediting/proofreading

» Formatting
» Cover art
» Ads
» Classes needed or resources purchased

Time Line
» Editing completed, all rounds
» Formatting
» Cover art

» Blog book tour or other online promotions

Marketing Plan
» Finishing up editing and formatting
» Setting up accounts on Amazon, Barnes & Noble, and Smashwords
» Setting up regular posts on several social networks at the same time
» Friends and family: Ask for reviews in exchange for free copies. Even bad reviews can boost sales! Show bad reviews of classic authors, such as Tolkien.
» Blog tour:
  – What blogs feature your type of book? J. A. Konrath (www.jakonrath.com) offers very frank advice and encouragement for self-publishing. Subscribe to authors you admire.
  – Advice from Anne O'Connell: www.summertimepublishing.com/blogging/ten-steps-to-a-successful-virtual-blog-tour-guest-post-from-anne-oconnell
  – Bringing the blog to you! Using guest authors on your blog to maximize promotions and save time
  – Setting a time line for publication and marketing
  – Thank-yous to hosts, guest authors
» Offering free sample pages from recent writing project to whet appetite
» Determining costs and value of postcards or other types of print promotions (rather than online)
» Release month should include daily or weekly promotion on social media, such as Facebook parties

Resources

Amazon self-publishing: https://kdp.amazon.com/self-publishing/help?topicId = A37Z49E2DDQPP3

Angela James's Before You Hit Send editing class (sign up for her newsletter on self-editing, too!): http://nicemommy-evileditor.com/before-you-hit-send/

Barnes & Noble Nook Press: https://www.nookpress.com

Calibre e-book management: http://calibre-ebook.com/demo

CreateSpace: www.createspace.com

Creating and selling an audiobook: http://blog.marketingtipsforauthors.com/2011/03/create-and -sell-audio-book-using-these.html

Digital Book World's directory of editorial and content services: www.digitalbookworld.com/ directory/editorial-services/

Directory of cover artists: http://voxiemedia.com/help-i-need-an-ebook-cover-designer/

Editorial Freelancers Association: www.the-efa.org

Lori Devoti's article on formatting from Word: http://howtowriteshop.loridevoti.com/2010/11/ how-to-format-ebook-word/

Mary DeMuth (you may choose to print out this excellent article for program attendees, mentioning that book promotion sites change in popularity and this article is a bit older): www.marydemuth.com/publish-your-e-book-in-seven-simple-steps/

Mobipocket creator: www.mobipocket.com/en/downloadsoft/productdetailscreator.asp

Smashwords: www.smashwords.com/about/how_to_publish_on_smashwords

CLUBS THAT KEEP THEM COMING BACK

CONGRATULATIONS! You have a group of passionate patrons who keep coming to programs on a particular topic or theme. Now what? Continue to feed their interest by turning one event into a quarterly or monthly club. Club meetings can be run in a similar way each session, with a new activity to inspire members. Patrons can register for one event or come to all of them, depending on space constraints. Having clubs can be easier on library staff for several reasons. First, the patrons will plan on the meeting date and time, especially if it is a monthly event. Second, the topics will begin to advertise themselves as patrons look for information on that club in the brochures and online and mention it to friends who have the same interests. Staff will get a feel for who is coming and how much interest is sustained by the topic. Third, supplies from one session can often be used again at another meeting.

The challenge for leading a passionate group is to keep ahead of new interests and trends. This chapter provides ideas for ten different clubs. Rather than presenting each program separately, this chapter provides ideas for club meetings. Topics and ideas covered here are designed for sessions lasting forty-five minutes to one hour and should not require a lot of setup or supplies. Outside speakers are sometimes suggested, but alternative ideas are provided as well.

Details for club activities are provided under the following headings.

SUGGESTED AGE RANGE

Each club has a suggested age range.

CLUB CONNECTIONS

In this section we list recurring features for each meeting of the club. For example, members of the 5K Club would discuss any races they attended and promote any they are registered for in future months.

IDEAS FOR SESSIONS

Topic ideas for ten meetings or sessions are provided.

CROSSOVER PROGRAMS

Other programs listed in this book might have topical crossovers that would work with this club. For example, the Fit Fair in the January chapter would be ideal for members of the 5K Club, or elements of the Fit Fair could be incorporated into meetings of the 5K Club.

VARIATIONS

Variations for different age groups when appropriate are provided, along with potential online components.

POWER PROMOTION

This section lists targeted marketing tips for each club.

5K CLUB

Many people have running a 5K or a marathon as a bucket list item and use races as a way to inspire themselves to get into shape. There are also plenty of people who run races often and are looking for information about new events and ways to keep the process exciting. A 5K club brings new and seasoned racers together to share information and tips. More important, it offers camaraderie and motivates members to keep going.

SUGGESTED AGE RANGE
30s–40s

CLUB CONNECTIONS

Each meeting can start with members mentioning any races they have completed and evaluating the course, crowd, prizes, and overall experience. Members in attendance can also discuss any upcoming events for which they are registered.

At the first meeting patrons attend, offer water bottles and pedometers as welcome gifts and inspiration to keep going with their fitness journey.

Members who have run or walked their first 5K can receive an inexpensive medal, and celebrating other milestones, such as completing five races or a longer race, can help motivate club members to keep returning.

IDEAS FOR SESSIONS

1 | **Area 5K Overview:** The first meeting of the year may feature an overview of all area races. Courses, fees, and rules change, and going over the local events, including pictures and details, will help racers plan their training and goals. The leaders can give this presentation formally, or each member can take a race and discuss it. Invite hosts of local races to talk to the club about their event.

2 | **Intro to Weight Training:** Those new to gyms are often daunted by weight equipment. The meeting can convene off-site for this session at a local park district or gym, or a trainer can bring photos of equipment and discuss which machines help with what types of strength training. The speaker can discuss which exercises are good for which age groups, as well.

3 | **Great Gyms:** Representatives from local gyms and fitness centers can discuss the features of each place or offer a 10-minute demo from some of the classes. Or the group can meet for prearranged tours at a few different sites throughout the month.

4 | **Fitbits and Other Technology Training:** Bring a Fitbit, Map My Run, and other apps for club members to look at and discuss. Pull information on new fitness gadgets to discuss in a presentation if it is not possible to look at them in hand. Invite members to discuss their favorite exercise apps.

5 | **From 0 to 5K:** Ask members who have run for a while to advise newer members about how to get started exercising. Emphasize that all people should check with their own doctors before starting a program. This is simply a positive discussion showing that it is possible even for those who have not exercised in a while to get started with a program. Library resources on simple exercises or on getting started with a walking plan can also be featured.

6 | **Virtual 5K and Charitable Exercising or Stair Climbing:** Area charity races or stair-climbing events are the theme of this club meeting. If the club has been operating for a while, members may want to host an event with a local park district or sponsor one that may benefit the library. But at this meeting, members will discuss virtual apps, including www.charitymiles.org or www.willrunforbling.com, by which exercise and steps help charities.

7 | **Map My Library Visits:** Using pedometers, members will enjoy a library scavenger hunt that includes the number of steps from the parking lot to the checkout desk or to the exercise DVD section. At the end of the hunt, offer healthy snacks or provide a yogurt parfait bar with yogurt and cereals or fruits.

8 | **From 5K to Marathon or Triathlon:** Assemble a panel of medical or training professionals to answer questions about the process of training for longer events. Club members who have gone through the process can also discuss what worked for them.

9 | **New Gear and Trends:** Engage a fitness trainer or encourage club members to discuss home exercise equipment, such as simple weights and bands. Members can each bring in a piece they enjoy using and discuss it with the group. Members can try the different pieces of equipment by doing, for example, simple stretches on the Swiss ball or kicks with the rubber bands.

10 | **Awards and Annual Wrap-Up:** At the end of the year, celebrate the achievements of members. From learning new exercises to walking in their first 5k, members should be recognized in some way with inexpensive medals or trophies. Each person can set some New Year's fitness goals, and members can brainstorm topics they would like to cover in next year's meetings.

CROSSOVER PROGRAMS

The January Fit Fair would appeal to many people training for a 5K, or members of this club may volunteer to help run that event.

VARIATIONS

» Virtual 5K Club: Running and walking are often solitary activities. Busy people like positive communities to keep their momentum going. Dedicate a section of library social media to 5Ks in the area. Invite patrons to join the social networking group and discuss upcoming events or post pictures from events. Offer Virtual 5K Club members a T-shirt with the library logo or a water bottle to use at events.

POWER PROMOTION

» Estimate the number of steps from the parking lot's farthest point to the checkout desk at the library and post a sign indicating how much exercise patrons are getting with that walk. Provide 5K Club information nearby.
» Feature upcoming races on library social media along with 5K Club meetings and be sure to emphasize that the club is for people at all stages of fitness.

YOUNG ADULT BOOKS FOR YOUNGISH ADULTS CLUB

This niche book club is an opportunity to reminisce as well as to explore themes in Young Adult literature with an adult perspective. Young Adult literature covers a variety of topics, such as diversity and sexual identity, that are relevant no matter a reader's age.

SUGGESTED AGE RANGE
20s–30s

CLUB CONNECTIONS

Young Adult (YA) and Teen books have proven their popularity not just with their intended audience but with readers of all ages. This book discussion group is intended for readers who have ostensibly aged out of Teen and YA literature, but who still love reading it just the same. This judgment-free zone will allow readers to discuss what they love about the genre as a whole as well as specific titles that the group reads together.

IDEAS FOR SESSIONS

1 | **Movie Tie-ins:** Movie versions of popular YA novels are a nearly constant presence at the box office. If your group decides to read a novel that is being made into a film, it presents the bonus opportunity of organizing a group outing to the theater to view and discuss the film.

2 | **Dystopian Novels:** There is no shortage of dystopian YA novels. Delve deeper than *The Hunger Games* and *Divergent* to find an under-the-radar title for your group to try out.

3 | **Graphic Novels:** Comic books and graphic novels continue to prove their popularity across age groups, and there are plenty of Teen- and YA-focused titles to choose from.

4 | **YA Classics:** Although there is a great possibility that some of your readers will have already read the book(s) chosen, chances are they haven't picked up something like *The Outsiders* or *The Giver* in quite some time. Plus, it's a great opportunity for readers who might have missed a classic YA title amid all their school-required reading.

5 | **Banned Books:** Banned Books Week takes place each September, and though there is certainly overlap between this theme and YA classics, there are also plenty of books added to the list of frequently challenged books each year.

6 | **Memoirs:** Whether a writer is a teen chronicling the challenges and triumphs of his life or an adult reflecting upon her adolescence, memoirs with a YA bent are often insightful, inspirational, and great material for discussion.

7 | **Paranormal Romance:** Though this particular YA genre is perhaps waning in popularity now, there are still plenty of *Twilight*-inspired titles available for lighter YA reading.

8 | **Science Fiction/Fantasy:** Although dystopian fiction and paranormal romance have already been listed, there are tons of read-worthy science fiction and fantasy YA novels that deal with neither and instead explore different worlds and mythologies.

9 | **Nonfiction:** The YALSA Award for Excellence in Nonfiction is a great place to start looking for excellent nonfiction YA titles that are not necessarily memoirs or biographies.

10 | **LGBT:** Sexual identity is dealt with in a variety of ways in YA literature, and novels with this theme present a great opportunity for discussion.

CROSSOVER PROGRAMS

Several other programs listed in this book might have topical crossovers and work with this programming series. For example, Great Reads and Treats for Book Clubs in the January chapter and Delicious Reads in the November chapter could easily be integrated into a book club meeting.

VARIATIONS

» Create a group on social media (for example, Goodreads or Facebook) for your book club so that readers will have a chance to carry on discussions outside group sessions.

» Also consider throwing a New Adult book into the mix. The New Adult genre is geared toward the post-YA group, and therefore it should prove interesting to read and discuss a New Adult title within the context of a group whose focus is primarily YA.

POWER PROMOTION

» Consider holding your book club meetings at an off-site location such as a local coffee shop or wine bar. Both are inviting spaces for book clubs and lend themselves well to relaxed conversation.

» As with Trivia Nights, this club will make for great, mutually beneficial community partnerships that can also increase your opportunities for promoting to possible participants who perhaps do not spend a lot of their time at the library. Area coffee shops or cafés are often filled with writers and readers with books or laptops who may be interested in library services.

TRIVIA NIGHTS

Pub trivia has become hugely popular in recent years, and it is an ideal program to be put on by a library. It presents a great opportunity for community partnerships as well as out-of-the-library programming.

There are many ways to approach an off-site pub trivia program series, but an ideal place to start is by partnering with a local restaurant or bar in order to put on the program. The goal is not just to find a place that you can use for your trivia night; rather, it is to find an establishment that can benefit from your presence, too.

SUGGESTED AGE RANGE
20s–30s

CLUB CONNECTIONS

This is an example of how to run a Trivia Night but is by no means the only way to do it. This setup will take about 1½–2 hours, so bear that in mind and adjust accordingly, if necessary.

» Each night includes six rounds, with five questions each round.
» Read all five questions before allowing time for players to write their answers. Repeat each question once or twice, then give several minutes for answering.
» If you have the means, incorporate music and create a playlist for the event. Play one or two songs while players are writing their answers, and let them know at what point (after the first song, after the second song, etc.) they will have to turn in their answers for scoring.
» An easy scoring method is to assign one point for each correct answer in round one, two points for round two, three points for round three, and so on.
» For added excitement you can offer a bonus round, in which teams will be given the bonus round category and then be able to wager their accumulated points *Jeopardy*-style before being given the bonus question.

PRO-TIP Don't spend too much time racking your brain to come up with thirty (or however many) trivia questions each month. There are tons of websites that provide free pub trivia questions. No matter what means you use to come up with questions, make sure to keep a record of the questions you ask so as not to have dreaded repeats!

IDEAS FOR SESSIONS

Depending on how many rounds you're going to incorporate into each Trivia Night, it is probably best—if you are interested in choosing themes—to apply themes to rounds rather than to the entire night. For example, some patrons might be turned off at the idea of an entire evening of sports trivia, but are willing to stick out one round that focuses on sports. Alternatively, if Olympics fever is sweeping the country, consider integrating a sports theme throughout the evening as opposed to asking specific sports questions (for example, you could ask questions about sports books and movies, sports figures that are infamous in popular culture, and important historical events related to sports).

1 | **Music:** Questions can focus on prominent figures in music, song titles, and missing lyrics. If you have the means, introduce a multimedia element and play snippets of songs that you're asking about instead of simply describing them or reading the lyrics.

2 | **Movies:** Questions can involve names of characters and actors and actresses, titles of films, and little-known movie facts. As with the music option, this is a great opportunity to show movie clips or play audio snippets to accompany the questions.

3 | **Focus on a Decade:** Ask questions relating to the important social, political, and pop culture events of a particular decade.

4 | **Sports:** As previously mentioned, questions about sports are not limited to the who, what, when, and where of events in sports history. You can also include questions about sports in movies, books, music, and television.

5 | **History:** Be careful about asking too many "On what date . . ." questions just because this is a history round. Make sure to include the whos, whats, and wheres also.

6 | **Geography:** Similar to number 5, don't fall into the habit of just asking "where" when creating geography-themed questions.

7 | **Books:** How can a library program not ask book-related questions? Again, this doesn't have to strictly involve questions about characters and plot settings, but can also involve movie tie-ins and the cultural significance of particular books.

8 | **Current Events:** It's up to you to decide how current your current events will be, but if you really want to keep participants on their toes and see who was paying attention to the news, you can ask questions that are specific to the past year or even month. It might sound like a gimme, but you'll probably be surprised!

9 | **Science/Technology:** This is one of the broadest categories provided here and can involve anything from the periodic table of elements to the latest iPhone.

10 | **Pop Culture:** This is something of a catchall theme that can incorporate any of the preceding themes as well as particularly notable fads and culture-defining moments.

CROSSOVER PROGRAMS

Several other programs listed in this book might have topical crossovers and work with this programming series. For example, '80s Night in the April chapter and '90s Night in the May chapter both lend themselves well to trivia. If you are doing either of those programs and it occurs later in the month than your Trivia Night, consider including a decade round with '80s or '90s trivia in order to promote your upcoming program. Or, focus your entire Trivia Night on either decade in order to get your patrons excited for an '80s or '90s night at the library. You can also feature trivia challenges at these programs as well as at programs such as the Shark Week Celebration in August or the Throwback Halloween Night in October.

VARIATIONS

If you are not able to offer your Trivia Night at an off-site location, that's okay! Provided your library has space, you can offer it there. If you are able to get clearance, consider offering it as an after-hours event.

POWER PROMOTION

» As mentioned, an important aspect of a Trivia Night is the off-site element. If you are partnering with a local restaurant or pub, ask to advertise the program in the space. Chances are you can, as it benefits the establishment as much as you.
» If the restaurant or pub is active on social media, see if the manager is willing to talk up your Trivia Nights there, as well.
» Speaking of social media, use your own library's social media to post information and teasers for upcoming Trivia Nights.
» Also consider asking whether the bar or restaurant manager is willing to provide gift cards or a round of drinks as a prize.

POWER PARENTING PROGRAM
PARENT NIGHTS

Parents know that bringing kids to the library is necessary, but often they do not realize everything the library has to offer them. In between taking kids to activities, parents of young children have few free nights or weekends to attend library programs. By offering a club where parents can bring young children or by offering it at the same time as a storytime or craft program that the kids can attend by themselves, you can provide parents a chance to talk to each other and learn about the library in a fun environment. Activities in this section are written with the assumption that young children will be playing near parents or in a corner of the room.

SUGGESTED AGE RANGE
30s–40s

CLUB CONNECTIONS

A program for parents with young children should keep logistics in mind. A meeting room close to washrooms that have changing stations saves time. Room for stroller parking outside or inside the room where they will not be in the way can help things go smoothly. Activities should be informal, and leaders should assume that parents will have to get up and deal with the needs of their children at times. Offering, or allowing parents to bring, healthy snacks like fruit, crackers, or cereals will enable everyone to stay longer at the program. The room could have a children's area set up with coloring books, washable markers or crayons, a table covering that is easy to clean, and puzzles.

Meetings can begin with introductions of children and parents. Leaders can introduce the subject and do a short demonstration of a library resource. Brief handouts will help parents remember the topic if they are managing young children at the same time. After the discussion of the topic, parents and children can try the equipment or visit with each other for the 45-minute session.

It is always a good idea to provide some handouts on getting a library card, current programs for all ages, and dates and subjects for future meetings. If a child gets upset or cries and the family needs to leave quickly, they will not have time to stop and get information on their way out the door. Having it handy in the room solves this issue.

Prepare to register members for summer and winter reading programs, including parents and children, before they leave the session at those times of the year. Many families do not realize programs are available for adults in addition to children.

IDEAS FOR SESSIONS

1 | **Downloadables:** Show parents how to download media from the website or use family-friendly databases like homework help and job searching resources. Play an audio children's story for the group. Some parents may wish to know how to download an e-book onto their phone or how to download an audio children's book onto another type of device, and, with staff help, they can go through the process here. Provide a couple of laptops so more than one person can work on this throughout the program.

2 | **Language Fun:** Bring in children's books in other languages or media on how to learn another language. Some libraries may subscribe to a database for this, and a short demonstration would be valuable. Parents from different cultures may not be aware of library materials in other languages. Provide information on English as a New Language classes in the area and resources on learning English.

3 | **Photo Booth and Frame Night:** Set up a laptop and printer. Discuss how to add money to library cards for printing in the library and go over options for computer and other equipment use for all ages in the library. Some libraries have equipment that can be reserved to convert videotapes to DVDs or to edit photos, music, and movies. If the library has that kind of equipment and classes, let parents know. Take and print digital photos of the families in the session, or have them do this for each other, showing them what types of paper to use and how to load the printer. Inexpensive craft kits for photo frames that children can decorate with markers or paint can be provided to go with the pictures.

4 | **Game Night and App Happy:** Show easy board and educational games for children, especially ones available for use in the library, keeping ones with small pieces away from the youngest children. Another option is to show educational apps and computer games for children. Printing simple BINGO cards off websites is another option. Families can take turns playing.

5 | **Healthy Snacking:** Provide a selection of library media on healthy cooking, especially children's cookbooks, for club members to peruse and check out. Samples of healthy snacks can be provided at this session, including, for example, the ingredients to make yogurt parfaits with fresh fruits, dried fruits, raisins, and cereals.

6 | **Meet the Board:** In many communities, the people on library boards are older or have older children and so are able to come to evening meetings. They may be a few years removed from the concerns of young children and young families, and it would be good for the two groups to meet each other and talk informally at a club session. Staff can facilitate introductions and question-and-answer sessions so that parents have a better understanding of how the library works and board members revisit their concerns. For example, parents may not know how policies are made in the library—for example, why more storytimes are not offered or why children under a certain age have to be attended at all times by people older than 18. Board members may need reminders of why stroller and parking accessibility is so important.

7 | **Shared Storytime:** Hold a storytime at this session and provide handouts of resources for simple songs, good books to read aloud, and crafts for families to try at home. Invite parents to share favorite activities or books they already read at home.

8 | **Power Puzzles:** Families can work together on puzzles at this event, or you can provide simple kits for making puzzles out of drawings. All sorts of puzzles can be offered from donations or library collections, ranging from floor-sized to simple 3-D building games. Many die-cutting machines have puzzle-making shapes. Word puzzles like Boggle or worksheets with word puzzles are also fun activities.

9 | **Career Recharge:** Introduce parents to career resources available through the library. Many parents may feel they need hours searching on the Internet while their child is next to them at the library when they actually have access to time-saving databases, résumé resources, and more. Handouts on local job fairs or trainings available at the library would be useful to parents who need to make a change or want a fresh start.

10 | **Travel Time:** Traveling with young children is daunting. Discuss day trips or have families discuss where they have been locally and some travel tips they have discovered. As always, library media on local or farther destinations should be easily available for members of the club to check out.

CROSSOVER PROGRAMS

This program can also be of interest to patrons attending the Ways to Work from Home event (see the August chapter) or the From Local Trips to Disney and Beyond—Tips for Traveling with Children forum (see the September chapter).

VARIATIONS

Simultaneous Storytime or Craft Workshop and Parent Event: If staff and space are available, offering a kids' program at the same time as Parent Nights allows the children to go into the next room. This would not work with children younger than preschool age, but it would offer parents a chance to focus on helpful information while their child is close by at a program. It can also keep parents from straying too far while younger children are in programs.

RETRO CRAFT CLUB

Everything old is new again at this club. Longtime crafters may know everything popular, but they may be too young to remember macramé and quilling. Going back over past favorite crafts can bring new techniques or embellishments to modern scrapbooking or needlework projects. This club does require some advance planning, shopping, and time to make samples, but projects should be easy enough that members can get an idea of the craft within a 45-minute session. Members will likely not finish a project each time and may opt to work more on one the next time or just learn a new technique each time. Members may request crafts or projects for future sessions.

SUGGESTED AGE RANGE
Older Teens–40s, or caregiver-child programs

CLUB CONNECTIONS

Members will start each meeting by introducing themselves and talking a bit about what types of crafts they like to do. Members may bring projects to show what they did since the previous session or what they are currently working on.

Show a video or demonstrate how to do a craft. If any club members know how to do a particular craft, solicit them to demonstrate at upcoming meetings.

Provide handouts with instructions or links. If supplies like looms are required, some club members may want to take one home to finish the project, as some will not be completed in the 45 minutes to 1 hour designated. This type of club could meet for 90 minutes, allowing members to work on their own projects and visit after the designated project.

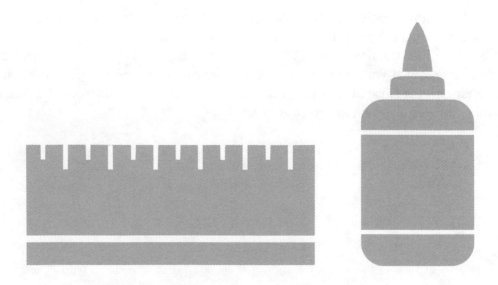

1 | Loopy for Looms

» When they were young, many people made oven mitts by weaving stretchy bands on looms. Members may enjoy revisiting this craft, though only one person can work on one loom at a time, and this project is time consuming. Bands, looms, and hooks need to be purchased from Amazon or craft suppliers such as Michaels. Kids' looms and kits are still available, and adults can easily work with those supplies, too.

» Look for potholder weaving videos on YouTube for a refresher, such as this one: http://youtu.be/gey7w5qzltU.

» For basic instructions, this is another good site: www.craftprojectideas .com/index.php/how-to/basic-techniques/1261-how-to-use-a-weaving -loom-to-make-a-potholder.

» Another type of loom that is fun for people to try is the flower loom. Popular in the '60s and '70s especially, these small, round looms can make flowers from raffia, ribbon, and even yarn. For this one, purchase yarn or darning needles with large eyes, yarn, and flower looms. These are available at craft stores, or vintage ones can be found in lots from eBay.

» This site has links to many basic instructions for different types of small looms: www.knitting-and.com/small-looms/#basic.

» The Hana-Ami Flower Loom tutorial uses flower looms sold currently in craft stores: http://youtu.be/MZJihs4shsc.

» Patrons can make several flowers in one session.

2 | Quilling

» The art of paper curling goes back to the 1700s. People would curl thin strips of paper or other materials around porcupine quills or needles. It can be easy to show patrons quilling by having them curl strips of origami or quilling paper (thin computer paper cut into ¼" strips works in a pinch) around pencils to practice. Have some card stock and glue sticks if club members want to glue shapes onto a card or bookmark.

» Aunt Annie's Crafts (www.auntannie.com/DecorativeCrafts/Quilling) is a good site for beginning quilling shapes, including how to glue shapes onto a card.

» The North American Quilling Guild (www.naqg.org) is a great resource.

3 | Three Cheers for Pom-Poms

» Pom-poms are among the easiest and most satisfying crafts to learn quickly. People can wind yarn around three fingers, then tie the bundle in the middle. After cutting the ends and shaping, crafters have a simple pom-pom. Craft stores offer fancy pom-pom makers, but these are not necessary. Popular in the '70s to tie on roller skates, pom-poms can also be tied together to make animals and more. For this activity, yarn, scissors, cardboard, and yarn or darning needles are all that is needed.

» This tutorial shows several methods for making pom-poms, including using simple cardboard discs: http://youtu.be/UcalLqkiqus.

» Goods Home Design's website (www.goodshomedesign.com/colorful -pompom-rug) has directions for several fun pom-pom projects, including a rug. They use a pom-pom maker for some of the ideas, but that is not necessary.

4 | Beaded Barrettes and Fascinators

» In the '80s, many young ladies wore barrettes woven with ¼" ribbon, beads, and feathers. Fascinators are confections made of felt or hair combs and feathers. All of these hair accessories are easy and fun to make.

» For the barrettes, purchase barrettes with parallel metal bars, ¼" ribbon in several colors, and scissors. Feathers and beads are optional, but can get heavy! Here is a tutorial on making these pretty pieces: http://youtu.be/ Cyhegv8K-jY.

» Here are some good, detailed instructions for ribbon streamer barrettes: www.xojane.com/diy/how-to-make-those-streamer-barrettes-from-your -70s-or-80s-childhood.

» Fascinators can simply be hair combs wrapped in ribbon with feathers, buttons, and ribbons attached. This site offers over 150 ideas: www .cutoutandkeep.net/projects/category/fashion/hair-accessories/fascinators.

5 | Iron Art

» Ironing beads into shapes is one vintage craft, and melting crayon shavings between sheets of waxed paper is another. Both of these have the potential to leave traces on the iron, so be prepared to clean it off with Magic Eraser or consider using a cheap portable iron for this type of project.

» For the bead project, patrons will need Perler fusible beads, parchment or waxed paper, a dry clothes iron set for no steam, and a pegboard. Here are some instructions for this activity: www.perlest.com.

» YouTube has a Perler Bead Planet channel, with many fun tutorials: www.youtube.com/channel/UCOdtKbKGWi42wlVOAlBaIzg.

» The Buggy and Buddy website (http://buggyandbuddy.com/crafts-for-kids -make-a-sun-catcher-with-crayon-shavings) has instructions for making a sun catcher with crayon shavings (or crayons grated with a food grater), waxed paper, construction paper frames, and string. This activity also uses a dry iron on a low, no steam setting.

6 | Iron-On Transfers

» In past decades, people would find iron-on transfers in the newspaper or on the backs of cereal boxes. Now, people can create them on the computer and print them on special transfer paper, ready for T-shirts, aprons, bags, and more.

» Club members can use clip art or other images to create their own transfers. HP, Avery, and other companies make iron-on transfer paper. As with the bead and crayon activities, irons need to be set for no steam. It is best to try this on small bags or with small designs first before making a large T-shirt design. Keep in mind that images need to be reversed so that they appear correctly on the final product. Be aware that transfer papers work only with inkjet printers and not laser printers.

» Here's a step-by-step guide: www.instructables.com/id/Iron-on-Transfers -for-T-Shirts-Tote-Bags-and-Oth/#step1.

7 | Seashells by the Sofa, Instead of by the Seashore

» Shell art was everywhere in the '70s, from ceiling nets to tissue box covers. Purchase simple, inexpensive wooden frames or boxes and shells from craft stores, along with craft glue. Crafters may elect to paint the frames a pretty color first in case any part shows through, before gluing on shells.

8 | Strung Out on String Art

» String art on velvet was another popular '60s and '70s trend, especially in owl designs. Basic string art involves fabric-covered wood and an outline made with nails, with spaces in between. Embroidery floss in various colors is looped around the nails to form a design.

» This site explores simple projects using everything from wood and nails to wire shapes covered in string: www.brit.co/diy-string-art.

» This site has thirty string art ideas, including a tree on a wall: www.architectureartdesigns.com/30-creative-diy-string-art-ideas.

9 | Plastic Canvas Party

» Plastic canvas allows crafters to easily make 3-D embroidery projects. Popular in past decades for everything from magnets to tissue box covers, plastic canvas projects are suitable for every skill level. With plastic canvas squares, yarn, scissors strong enough to cut plastic, yarn or darning needles, and magnet strips, crafters at this meeting could make a magnet in one session.

» Beginning stitch patterns are here: www.nuts-about-needlepoint.com/ painted-canvas-stitches.

» This site has lessons, tutorials, and simple patterns: www.allcrafts.net/ plcanvas.htm.

» Some craft stores have plastic canvas precut in shapes such as hearts or stars that crafters fill in with yarn stitches and edgings.

10 | Retro Ornaments or Gifts

» Simple paper angels or ornaments were very popular in past decades. A macramé wreath can introduce the macramé and latch hook techniques.

» From cracker boxes, crafters cut out a cardboard circle 1¾" in diameter. They then cut the center out of that circle, producing a ring that is ¼" wide.

» Next, crafters cut Lion Brand Homespun yarn into 4″ lengths (about 30 pieces will be needed). Each piece should be folded in half, making a loop. Wreath makers then put the loop inside the ring and pull the ends through the loop, covering the ring. A thin ribbon can be used to hang the ornament. Red pieces of yarn or berries can also be added.

» Additional easy and fun holiday crafts can be found at the following websites:
  – God's Eye: http://craftsbyamanda.com/2011/08/camp-crafts-gods-eye.html
  – Pom-Pom Bookmark: www.designmom.com/2012/10/the-perfect-gift-yarn-ball-bookmark
  – Quill Snowflakes: www.marthastewart.com/851883/quill-snowflakes
  – Woven Barrette: www.xojane.com/diy/how-to-make-those-streamer-barrettes-from-your-70s-or-80s-childhood
  – Folded Paper Angel Ornament: http://funezcrafts.com/Folded-Paper-Angel.html
  – Curled Paper Snowflake: www.hgtv.com/design/make-and-celebrate/entertaining/make-a-paper-snowflake-star-christmas-ornament
  – Muslin Angel Ornaments: http://dpeagreendesigns.blogspot.com/2009/10/muslin-angel-ornaments-inexpensive-way.html

CROSSOVER PROGRAMS

Decades programs like the '80s and '90s Nights (in the April and May chapters) could use some of these projects, as could the December program DIY Holiday Gifts and Decorations on the Cheap. The Crafterwork Club could easily incorporate these ideas and supplies as well.

VARIATIONS

Cheap and Quick Gifts: Several of the crafts mentioned for this club would work well for a drop-in gift making program. A card or bookmark quilling station, an ornament making area, and a pom-pom making table would be a good start.

POWER PROMOTION

» Make samples of projects for the next month and show them at the end of each meeting.
» Display samples with books and media on topical crafts to draw attention to upcoming meetings. Be sure to include a list of upcoming meeting dates.
» Ask local craft supply stores to post information about the group, especially if you purchase supplies at that location.
» Feature projects on the library social media sites or a Pinterest page and invite patrons to post their own.

CRAFTERWORK

Crafterwork is a club intended to bring together patrons who enjoy working on do-it-yourself projects and trying new forms of art. This monthly club gives patrons, whether they are novices or more dedicated crafters, an opportunity to experiment with different art mediums in a social environment.

SUGGESTED AGE RANGE
20s–30s

CLUB CONNECTIONS

After introductions, encourage members to share their skills with the group. Don't forget to always bring books from the collection to inspire new ideas.

IDEAS FOR SESSIONS

1 | **Knit Circle:** Chances are, if you work in a library, someone will know how to knit. Share your knowledge with the group and create scarves, tea cozies, or mittens. Encourage crafters to bring different sizes of needles and knit for others (for example, see the Hats for Newborns project of the Service Club discussed later in this chapter). Have alternative types of yarn arts available, such as needlepoint, loom weaving, or crochet.

2 | **Origami or Paper Folding:** Members can learn how to fold paper into different designs, such as roses. Provide discarded library books for cutting out pages to create a literary-themed garden of flowers.

3 | **Mason Jar Mod Podge:** Members can decorate glass bottles and mason jars with decorative paper from the craft store, maps, or even pages from old books. Mod Podge will adhere the paper to the bottles or jars, and accessories such as ribbons, stickers, and strings will create a unique look. Another option is to make fall-themed bottles or jars and decorate with autumn leaves instead of paper.

4 | **Wire Wrapping Jewelry:** Using needle-nose pliers, patrons wrap crafting wire (gold or silver) around pieces of sea glass or other gems. The sea glass can then be attached to a necklace chain. Other forms of wire wrapping can include rings, bracelets, and earrings.

5 | **Personalized Coffee Mugs:** Members use oil-based Sharpies to draw on and personalize coffee mugs. Patrons can take the mugs home to bake in their ovens (350 degrees, for 30 minutes, put in while cold) to set the design. Another option is to decorate wine glasses with Sharpie paint pens and have patrons bake them at 200 degrees for 1 hour.

6 | **Glass Etching:** Have patrons bring in their own glassware for this program. Some interesting items to etch are candy dishes, mason jars, cups, candlesticks, and the like. Crafters use a stencil or sticker to design what they would like etched on the glass. They adhere the stencil or sticker to the glass and use a paintbrush to put on the glass etching cream. After 10–15 minutes, the cream should be rinsed off. Make sure patrons wear gloves when handling the etching cream and rinsing off the glassware.

7 | **Scrapbooking:** Encourage patrons to bring photographs ahead of time, or provide a printer they can send cell phone pictures to. Provide a workstation filled with scissors, glue, stickers, block letters, embellishments, and different card stock images to celebrate important events—vacations, graduations, birthdays, weddings, holidays, and so on.

8 | **Pumpkin Decorating:** Provide mini pumpkins and a worktable of decorative accessories—feathers, ribbons, glitter, Sharpies, acrylic paints, and the like. This is a great opportunity to clean out your craft closet. A more traditional route is to purchase large pumpkins and carve them.

9 | **Polymer Clay Charms:** Patrons design simple or sophisticated charms for a keychain, a bracelet, or earrings using polymer clay. Crafters use a rolling pin to flatten the clay and a toothpick or the narrow tip of a paintbrush handle to help shape the charm. They then insert an eye pin and bake the charms in either a toaster oven or regular oven (time and temperature depend on the brand of clay). Patrons can get creative and fashion the clay into animals, shapes, foods, and fun objects such as coffee cups. Fimo clay can also be made into beads or pendants with designs carved into them.

10 | **Holiday Ornaments:** Patrons decorate the inside of clear glass ornaments with holly, pine needles, fake snow, tiny pinecones, and fake cranberries. Provide materials for the exterior as well: ribbons, glitter, Sharpies, and acrylic paints.

CROSSOVER PROGRAMS

Members of this club may also enjoy the Retro Craft Club. Some topics will also be of interest for the Social Justice and Activism program detailed in the March chapter and the Bonfire Night in September. The Service Club may also enjoy making these craft items and selling them to raise money for charitable organizations.

VARIATIONS

» Virtual: Have Pinterest or Instagram contests and encourage your patrons to pin their crafts to the library's pages. Use specific hashtags such as #librarycrafterwork or #libcrafting.
» Older Teens: Tie-dyeing and bleaching T-shirts are fun and simple ways to design useful and crafty outerwear. Tie-dyeing requires white T-shirts, a tie-dyeing kit, buckets of water, and rubber bands. Bleaching requires a colorful T-shirt, bleach, and a design that teens will essentially "bleach out." Make sure teens use gloves and eye protection!

POWER PROMOTION

» Yarn bomb the library and stick notes or flyers into the yarn promoting Crafterwork.
» Secure a display case for your patrons' Crafterwork artwork in the library. Show off samples of your club's work and encourage others to come. Make sure to include a list of upcoming meeting dates.

RETRO MOVIE NIGHT

Retro has a somewhat specific meaning here, as the session ideas involve movies that are primarily from the '80s and '90s, with a few from the '70s. The intent is to celebrate the cultural touchstones of your patrons. Depending on where patrons fall on the age spectrum, the movies they consider "classics" from their childhood will vary. For example, someone who came of age in the early '80s might not consider a children's movie from the early '90s to be relevant to him. Luckily this series presents plenty of opportunities to reach all your Millennial patrons.

SUGGESTED AGE RANGE
20s–30s

CLUB CONNECTIONS

A great way to bring people together is through the shared experience of watching movies. A monthly Retro Movie Night is a low-key but endlessly entertaining way to bring people together. It's not possible to list every movie that you could incorporate into this kind of programming, but we've listed several here, as well as popular movie categories, to give you a jumping-off point.

IDEAS FOR SESSIONS

1 | **RomCom:** *When Harry Met Sally; The Sure Thing*
2 | **School Days:** *The Breakfast Club; Fast Times at Ridgemont High; Dazed and Confused*
3 | **Horror:** *Texas Chainsaw Massacre; Friday the 13th; Nightmare on Elm Street; Halloween*
4 | **Science Fiction:** *2001: A Space Odyssey; Alien; Star Wars*
5 | **Box Office Smashes:** *Jaws; Jurassic Park; The Matrix*
6 | **Animation Celebration:** *The Lion King; Toy Story; Who Framed Roger Rabbit?*
7 | **So Bad They're Good (or Not . . .):** *Twister; Independence Day; The Mummy*
8 | **Friends Forever:** *Now and Then; The Goonies; Stand by Me*
9 | **Childhood Revisited:** *The NeverEnding Story; The Mighty Ducks; Honey, I Shrunk the Kids; The Karate Kid; E.T.*
10 | **Season's Greetings:** *National Lampoon's Christmas Vacation; A Christmas Story; Home Alone*

CROSSOVER PROGRAMS

Several other programs listed in this book might have topical crossovers and work with this programming series. For example, '80s Night in the April chapter and '90s Night in the May chapter both lend themselves well to movie nights, as does Throwback Halloween Night in October. Oscar Night in the February chapter also presents a great chance to cross over. If you are planning to put on an Oscar Night program, consider choosing a past Oscar winner for your Retro Movie Night that month.

VARIATIONS

» Movie-oke Night: Hold a night of movie-oke! Many favorite films of the '70s, '80s, and '90s are also endlessly quotable, so invite your attendees to test their memories as well as their acting chops with movie scene karaoke. Lessen the burden on your crowd by inviting a local movie-oke troupe to assist in the performance.
» Film Series: Consider doing a series of films, such as a summer series, in which you show a different summer film at your June, July, and August film nights. This can also be done with a movie series (for example, three months of *Back to the Future*).

POWER PROMOTION

» Place flyers in your library's AV department—near the movies, of course.
» If you're putting on any of the aforementioned crossover programs (or other programs that you feel cross over), be sure to talk up your movie nights there, too!

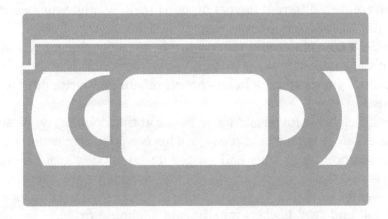

COMMUNITY COLLEGE CONNECTIONS

Establishing a bond with your local community college will help keep the public library in many high school grads' minds. Many students get caught up in the whirlwind of homework and do not reenter the public library until after they have graduated from college, or even after having children of their own. Offer a balance of 10- to 15-minute drop-in programs and some traditional programming that establishes a connection between the library and the college.

SUGGESTED AGE RANGE
Older Teens–20s

CLUB CONNECTIONS

Depending on the setting, meetings can be run a few different ways but should always begin with patrons introducing themselves so they have a chance to talk about what they are studying. Then a theme or activity is introduced. Name tags will help with the drop-in events.

IDEAS FOR SESSIONS

1 | **Hot Chocolate Tasting:** Set different types of hot chocolate mixes on a table with various toppings. Popular flavors and toppings include peppermint, caramel, vanilla, hazelnut, different flavors of marshmallow, and whipped cream. Poll the popular flavors and mixings throughout the day.

2 | **Un-Valentine's Day:** No pretty pink or purple hearts at this party—only black! Decorate the room with black and gray, play dark and brooding music to greet guests. Allow guests to hit a heart-shaped piñata and write out mean villain-tine cards.

3 | **Book Party:** Celebrate loved and hated books at this book party. Be sure to advertise advance copies or giveaways. This is a good opportunity to share information about the library and gauge interest about starting a book club. Use this as a trial run and see what types of books students are interested in reading.

4 | **Mini Flowerpot Decorating:** Decorate mini flowerpots with Sharpies or paint. Provide soil and seed packets for students to choose from.

5 | **LEGO Build Night:** Bring in LEGOs and encourage students to play and build with them in the lounge or student center during breaks. The power of play and creativity cannot be understated, and providing LEGOs is a great way to inspire others. An alternative idea is to have a contest for building roller coasters out of paper towel tubes.

6 | **Trivia:** Host an afternoon trivia contest with prizes for first, second, and third places. Participants may want to play as individuals as opposed to teams, and rounds may have to be shorter to fit the time frame of class schedules. Choose a theme ("I Love the '80s" or "Classic TV Shows") to go with certain rounds.

7 | **Soda Tasting Contest:** Set out different types of soda and ask people to identify the brand. Keep a tally on a whiteboard of the number of students who can tell the difference.

8 | **Karaoke Night:** Let it go and sing out loud to your favorite songs! Grab a karaoke machine, a laptop and TV, a microphone, and karaoke CDs from the library, and you're ready to go. Advertise a fun evening of laughs and snacks to go along with this program.

9 | **Charlie Brown Thanksgiving:** Show *A Charlie Brown Thanksgiving* in the student lounge. Serve classic food inspired by the movie: pretzels, jellybeans, and popcorn.

10 | **DIY Stress Ball:** Help students relax in the busy weeks before finals by having them create stress balls. Students use a funnel to pour rice or flour into a balloon and securely knot it. They then place a second or even third balloon over the entire stress ball to cover it for support. If possible, brand the balloons with the library logo and write "good luck" or other encouraging sayings.

CROSSOVER PROGRAMS

Topics from other programs featured in this book would also appeal to the patrons attending this club. Both the Hot Drink Mixology and Un-Valentine's Day programs in the February chapter would translate well for this crowd. The March Madness event will attract college students' attention as they prepare for the basketball season playoffs. Technology makes a Karaoke Night (see the August chapter) easy to offer at a satellite location such as a community college. The topics from the Crafterwork and Young Adult Books for Youngish Adults clubs would also appeal to older teens in this group.

VARIATIONS

» Student Open House: Invite students to an open house at the public library to show them what resources and fun programs are available. If the community college has an open house or library instruction classes, ask to participate and get involved. Work with the community college librarians to arrange this.

» Online: Create a March Madness bracket for local sports teams or favorite books. See the March Madness program for more ideas.

POWER PROMOTION

» Select an unexpected location. These programs often work best if offered in a hallway or a busy area of campus.

» Offer programs during prime school hours and don't forget to brand all your items.

» Work with the community college librarians to establish ideal days, times, and activities.

WRITERS' WORKSHOP

Writers often look to the library as a resource on how to get published or work on their craft. Feedback and critiques are essential for writers. Today's authors also need information on publishing, marketing, and trends so that their work will be marketable when they are ready for that step. This club should be age specific. Issues important to younger writers will be different from those of more seasoned adults.

SUGGESTED AGE RANGE

Separate for Older Teens–20s and 30s–40s
(If patrons outside the advertised age group are interested in forming a writing group, consider offering more sessions, including one for seniors.)

CLUB CONNECTIONS

Meetings should begin with introductions. Each member could discuss what she likes to write and where she is in her writing career. New members often feel less shy when they meet people at all levels, from beginners to those who have had some work published.

An icebreaker writing activity is a good way to start the meeting. Consider asking participants to write a haiku, a tweet describing their latest project, or a progressive story (one person writes one sentence before passing it on to the next person).

Collect names of everyone who would like to share work for critique that meeting. If there are more than six, consider drawing randomly and asking for e-mail volunteers to critique the work of any member who does not get to read (these virtual critiques should be done before the next meeting). Members may also enjoy virtual feedback in between sessions, especially if meetings are monthly or fewer. Set guidelines for critiques, such as three pages for fiction and five to eight minutes for comments from the audience. Some writers may opt to stay only for the theme portion of the evening and not for the critiquing.

Themes for sessions can be done at the beginning of the meeting, allowing time for sharing and critiquing. To save time, e-mail the theme to members or tell them ahead of time so they can bring in samples.

Members who are too harsh with critiques or who spend too much time asking questions about their own work may crop up in a writing group. A general announcement about keeping comments positive yet helpful and making sure everyone speaks who wants to is one way to minimize the negative commenters' impact. Those who want to spend lots of time discussing their individual project or writing concerns should be directed to library resources or invited to visit the reference desk to find more resources particular to their needs.

IDEAS FOR SESSIONS

1 | Planning the Writing Year: The January meeting could inspire members to plan writing projects for the year. Goals may include entering a contest, pitching a story, or finishing or publishing a project. The group could write down their goals, and some may want to share.

2 | Not So Lovely Poems: Turn Valentine's Day upside down with Not So Lovely Poems. Invite club members to write unromantic poetry. Switch it up by asking for rhyming poems, couplets, or other variations. Pull some fun and quirky read-alouds such as works by Shel Silverstein.

3 | Fresh Flash Fiction: This trend is appearing in many writing venues that ask for submissions and in contests. Invite members to write by themselves with a 100- to 1,000-word limit. Use a theme such as books or the library for inspiration. Go over guidelines, such as maintaining a balance between dialogue and narration and creating as complete a storyline as possible. Ask if anyone would like to share the result.

4 | Contests and Pitching: Invite members to share information about contests they have entered and how those contests worked. Pull information on romance, science fiction, or mystery contests online. Last, give members an opportunity to practice an elevator pitch of their latest project—that is, a summary in a couple of sentences.

5 | Queries: Provide samples of query letters from library books. Invite members to write a quick query letter about their latest project for an agent or publisher, then share and critique.

6 | Staging a Scene: Screenwriting takes the stage at this meeting, where participants are invited to write a short scene on a theme. Scenes should include character placement, action, and dialogue. Invite members to take parts of some of the scenes and act them out.

7 | Plotting a Murder in an Hour: At this meeting, members will brainstorm the characters, plot, setting, and more for a murder mystery. Provide a whiteboard and use sticky notes for easy rearranging of characters or changes in plot. The intent is to show basic plotting of introduction, action, pinnacle, and conclusion and to inspire writers to plot an entire project quickly before getting down to the writing.

8 | Memoirs: Ask members to write a scene about a significant event in their lives and share. Display library copies of memoirs and perhaps read some sections. Another option is to play some of Frank McCourt's reading of *Angela's Ashes*.

9 | Nonfiction: Pull copies of Writer's Guides with nonfiction markets and provide samples of cookbooks, business books, how-to books, and other types of nonfiction guides members may be interested in. Pull nonfiction, prize-winning titles and read samples of some pages aloud to highlight pacing and other techniques that bring nonfiction subjects to life.

10 | Business of Writing: Ask writers to share their experiences with marketing, planning appearances, filling out tax forms for writing income, and more. Pull library materials on the business aspects of writing.

CROSSOVER PROGRAMS

Either the Poetry Reading Night in April, the NaNoWriMo Kickoff and Weekly Write-Ins in November, or the Smart Tips for Self-Publishing program in December will have topics and activities attractive to members of this group.

VARIATIONS

Online: An online writing group may be easier for those who want to critique and have their work critiqued. Members could be part of a closed Facebook group or be managed through e-mail or a Yahoo! group. Send links or lists of library materials related to the topics and themes. Ask members to write poetry or scenes or do many of the activities described in the Ideas for Sessions section for live meetings.

SERVICE CLUB

Many people are looking for ways to give back to the library and community, but they don't have the time or means to become a part of the library's Friends group. A Service or Volunteer Club with dedicated monthly programs is a low-key way to have a core group of volunteers and vigilant, young supporters of the library.

SUGGESTED AGE RANGE
20s–40s

CLUB CONNECTIONS

Begin meetings with an update on current and upcoming projects. Share positive reactions from organizations, along with any feedback about needs for new items.

IDEAS FOR SESSIONS

1 | **Random Acts of Kindness:** Members write kind thoughts and affirmations on small pieces of card stock or stationery (for example, "You can do it!" "Be yourself because you're amazing," and "Just read and relax—everything is going to be okay"). Place these in library books in all departments for a nice surprise when someone checks out a book.

2 | **Hats for Newborns:** Many hospitals and shelters need donations of baby items. If you have talented knitters in your group, encourage them to knit baby hats for newborns or premature babies. This is also a good way for members to teach new skills to one another and to enjoy socialization and camaraderie.

3 | **Senior Center Game Night:** Arrange a day and time with a local senior center for club members to visit residents for an hour or two of socializing and playing board games. This is a great way to encourage intergenerational programming and to make senior citizens feel valued.

4 | **Flower Planting:** April showers bring May flowers, and spring is the perfect time to beautify the library and surrounding areas. Plan a day of planting with flowers from local shops (ask shops and nurseries to donate plants or to sponsor the event if cost is a concern).

5 | **E-mail Campaign:** Members can show support and appreciation for the library by sponsoring an e-mail writing campaign to the mayor, local representatives, or even Congress members. If your library is in danger of budget cuts, invite patrons to write about what the library means to them and their families and how it has helped their lives. This is an opportunity to advocate for libraries, educate patrons about funding, and even encourage them to run for the library board.

6 | **Bench Painting:** Many libraries have benches or outdoor seating areas for patrons. Invite members to decorate or paint one that is dedicated to the library and literacy. Another option is to help decorate a booth or float for the library in a local parade or fair.

7 | **Reading Buddies:** Although many libraries partner with Youth Services for reading buddies or Read to a Dog programs, this is a great opportunity to branch out to a different audience. If your library has a significant immigrant population or conversation club, why not encourage them to improve their reading skills by reading to a friend? Another option is to organize a trip to a local senior center or hospital to read to those who are homebound or unable to read. Members can work with your library's outreach librarian or department to better serve the community and to assess the needs of patrons.

8 | **Cards for Soldiers:** Support and acknowledge the hard work service members do overseas by inviting members to create thank-you cards or holiday greeting cards. Make sure your group does this well in advance of the holiday season because there are certain mailing deadlines. Several different organizations support this cause, including A Million Thanks (http://amillionthanks.org) and the American Red Cross (www.redcross.org/support/get-involved/holiday-mail-for-heroes).

9 | **Pet Toys for Animal Shelters:** Humans aren't the only ones who need love and affection—animals do, too! Invite members to create simple dog and cat pull toys for no-kill shelters out of fabric by knotting and braiding in easy patterns.

10 | **Food Donations:** Many libraries offer a Food for Fines program during the holiday season and need help organizing the food items donated by patrons. Host a night of packing and organizing for the Service Club to bring items to the local food pantry. If your library does not have a Food for Fines program, set up a time for your group to work at a local shelter or food pantry to help with its organizing needs.

CROSSOVER PROGRAMS

The Social Justice and Activism program, the Green Party, or the Seed Bomb and Terrarium DIY event, all in the March chapter, will appeal to members of this group.

VARIATIONS

» Online: Host a Virtual Service Club and have participants e-mail or log hours to the library. Participants can also tag the library when performing their service hours.
» Older Teens: Set a goal of a certain number of volunteer hours for the library's Teen Advisory Board to complete in one year. Throw a party at the end of the year upon completion.

POWER PROMOTION

» Advertise this club heavily at other events and programs for 20s and 30s.
» Encourage regular attendees to participate and even help organize events.

ABOUT THE AUTHORS

AMY J. ALESSIO is an award-winning, part-time teen librarian at the Schaumburg Township District Library in Schaumburg, Illinois. She recently wrote *Mind-Bending Mysteries and Thrillers for Teens: A Programming and Readers' Advisory Guide* for ALA Editions. Her first young adult mystery, *Taking the High Ground,* was published in 2013. She has enjoyed teaching online courses for YALSA (Young Adult Library Services Association) and webinars for ALA along with many live presentations. She has given many talks on vintage cookbooks based on her passion, featured at www.amyalessio.com. To feed her book addiction, she reviews teen and adult books for *Crimespree Magazine* and *Booklist* magazine.

KATIE LaMANTIA is an award-winning teen librarian at the Schaumburg Township District Library in Schaumburg, Illinois. A former Teen Advisory Board member and current teen librarian and 20–30-something, she has a personal as well as a professional interest in serving the needs of this demographic. She has presented at multiple state and national library conferences about libraries, teens, and technology. When not running teen programs, tinkering with technology, and finding amazing books for young adults, she enjoys reading, writing, traveling, and extreme adventure activities.

EMILY VINCI is a popular services librarian specializing in adult readers' advisory at the Schaumburg Township District Library in Schaumburg, Illinois. She has interests in expanding library appreciation and knowledge of comics and graphic novels, as well as catering to hard-to-reach demographics such as the 20s and 30s crowd. A pop culture fiend, she is always looking for new ways to incorporate popular culture into the public library.

INDEX